VISION:
LOST
AND
FOUND

"I've had a front-row seat to the undeniable transformation happening at Granger. *Vision: Lost & Found* tells the story of a church daring to question long-held paradigms and imagine a new way to impact their community. This isn't a book full of nicely packaged success stories—Tim Stevens reveals the good, the bad and the ugly of their journey. But I'm confident every church leader who reads this book will walk away thinking differently about their next steps."

—ALAN HIRSCH
Author of numerous award winning books on missional Christianity including *On The Verge, The Permanent Revolution,* and *The Forgotten Ways.* Founder of Forge Mission Training Network and co-leader of Future Travelers.

"*Vision: Lost and Found* is a fascinating and raw inside look at a church struggling to discover God's next assignment in a rapidly changing culture.

Anyone in leadership at a church going through a difficult transition can relate to Tim Stevens unblinking retelling of his gut-wrenching journey at one of the most recognizable churches in America. The beauty of *Vision: Lost and Found* is that Tim not only narrates the journey, but also gives practical tools for fellow travelers."

—GEOFF SURRATT
Director of Exponential

"Thank you, Tim Stevens for *Vision: Lost and Found.* Thank you for giving the reader a "front row seat" to Granger Community Church's extraordinary 25 year journey of "helping people take their next step toward Christ...together." Tim Stevens is an exceptionally gifted leader as Executive Pastor of one of America's most innovative churches. He is also a great visionary leader of church leaders around the world.

Whether your church is large or small, young or old, traditional or contemporary, "missional" or "attractional", there are practical ideas, proven processes, and helpful strategies in this book that can help your church "raise the bar" and take her next steps to more powerfully and effectively reach people for Christ. This is a must read for every church leader!"

—JOEL MIKELL
President, RSI Church Stewardship

"Church leaders today are addicted to product when real meaning is found through process. That's why Tim Stevens has just delivered a "must read." Honest and compelling, the story of Granger is one of the best snapshots of a visioning journey you will find. Dive in to refresh your own ministry dreams while basking in the pure sunshine of transferable insight."

—WILL MANCINI
Founder of Auxano, author of *Church Unique*

"With rare authenticity and genuine openness, *Vision: Lost and Found* tells the whole story of Granger Community Church. Tim Stevens courageously writes about the good times of dramatic growth and the challenging times of economic struggle, decline and blurred vision. In the process, Tim shares the hard work and heart work this team did to regain their vision, recalibrate and continue to have an impact not just in their community but around the world. Every church leader needs this book because the truth is, we have all been there or will be there at some point in our ministries."

—DAVE FERGUSON
Lead Pastor - Community Christian Church
Spiritual Entrepreneur – NewThing

VISION:
LOST
AND
FOUND

THE STORY OF A CHURCH THAT GOT STUCK
BUT DIDN'T STAY THERE

TIM STEVENS

Vision: Lost and Found

Copyright © 2012 by Tim Stevens in partnership with Exponential Resources

ISBN-13: 978-1475033298
ISBN-10: 147503329X

Exponential Resources
P.O. Box 2024
Centreville, VA 20122
(800) 319.5361
exponential.org

This book is manufactured in the United States.

Credits
Cover Design: Dustin Maust
Interior Design: Brittany Riblet
Copy Editor: Amanda Harris

Other books by Tim Stevens
Simply Strategic Stuff: Help for Leaders Drowning in the Details of Running a Church
Simply Strategic Volunteers: Empowering People for Ministry
Simply Strategic Growth: Attracting a Crowd to Your Church
Pop Goes the Church: Should the Church Engage Pop Culture?

TO PATRICK MCGOLDRICK

You've told me the story of how you met Jesus. A small rural church in Sharon, Pennsylvania, made the introduction, and it changed your life forever. Your dreams changed and you headed off to college to study the Bible and learn how to lead a church. It was there that you met my sister, and not long after, we became friends.

As your brother-in-law, I've watched you live out your faith. I've seen you treat my sister with love and respect, and I've taken notes as you've raised two amazing children into the man and woman of God they are today. I've seen your leadership in action from afar, and know there are hundreds of people around the world today who are aggressively pursuing their faith as a result of having you as their youth pastor.

When I sat with you a few months ago just after you learned you have ALS, a terminal illness, I could not imagine the utter sense of despair and helplessness you must have felt. I know you have good days and bad days, but what I've seen since that day is a man who didn't flee his faith. Your faith in the most unimaginable of situations has strengthened my faith.

Your faith is the reason I'm still involved in church. The work of a church is way too hard to stay in it without some sense of purpose. I truly believe that the Church—the way God intended it to be—is our only hope when the fragility of life comes crashing down. Your response to this disease, which we are told will take your life within a few short years, can only be explained by your faith in Jesus.

And so I continue to pursue the vision of helping as many people as possible take steps toward Jesus. This book, which I dedicate to you, is another attempt to help churches do better. For if every church does a little bit better at helping people grow into mature, reproducing disciple-makers, then we might just see His kingdom come here on earth, even as it is in heaven.

Tim Stevens

CONTENTS

ACKNOWLEDGEMENTS

Mark Beeson

Your leadership through our 18 years together has been unbelievable. You have always been more interested in my success than your own. You knew writing was my passion and made room in the schedule for me to regularly get away and write. This book is a result of that priority.

Granger Community Church

This book is your story! The testimony of your faith, innovation, willingness to risk and trust in God has been told all over the world time and again. Thousands of churches are more effective because you've allowed them to learn from you.

Faith

My precious wife. Since you are an extrovert, it's probably hard to understand why I like to sit in a dark corner for hours and write. But you give me the space—and I am so grateful! I can't imagine life without you by my side. Thank you for being such a great partner.

Heather, Megan, Hunter and Taylor

Can we just agree you are the most amazing kids on the planet? My life is better because you are all a part of it. I knew making kids would be fun, but who knew that having them around the house would be life-changing? Watching you each explore the world and take steps in your walk with Jesus is a delight that never gets old.

My Team   It should surprise no one that I'm pretty worthless by myself. A big thanks to my team who helped make this book happen, including Amanda Harris, Brittany Riblet, Dustin Maust, Jami Ruth, Kem Meyer, Mark Waltz, Jason Miller and Rob Wegner.

INTRODUCTION

I live in northern Indiana near the shores of Lake Michigan. Winter begins in early November and typically doesn't let up until late March. It's five months of howling winds and snowy roads. The weather systems come across from Chicago, pick up moisture off the relatively warm waters of the lake and dump it as snow on our walks and driveways. Last year over 110" of snow landed in our front yards.

I enjoy living in a place where there are four very distinct seasons. But winter gets extremely long. By early March, I'm usually wondering why I decided to live in such a place. Everything is dead, and the beauty of the white snow has long ago lost its appeal. The roads are dirty, yards are matted down, a season's worth of trash blows in the wind, curbs are torn up from the constant beating by the snow plows and streets are full of potholes from the cyclical freezing and thawing.

The thing that is particularly hard about March is that you can begin to smell spring, but it's still several weeks away. You know it's coming, but you still have to get up every day and look at the ugliness that winter left behind.

Yes, sometimes winter is way too harsh. And way too long.

We recently emerged from a harsh winter as a church. It was longer than five months. In fact, looking back, it was a five-year winter.

This long winter included a beating on church finances with a terrible recession and local unemployment among the highest in the country. At its worst, one out of every five people in our congregation no longer had a job.

Lost jobs meant lower offerings, which meant we had to eliminate several staff positions and cut hours of many others.

The hard winter also included strained relationships. In fact, for much of this time, I wasn't seeing eye-to-eye with my closest partner in ministry. It was killing me, and it was hurting the church.

I've spent hours thinking through the reasons for our long winter. Why did it happen? Why couldn't we avoid it? After 20 years of growth and vitality and life—why did the harshness of winter come so strong and stay so long? I can't blame the recession entirely. Many churches went through the same thing and yet were thriving. I can't blame the people around me. Anyone who visits knows we have one of the best teams on the planet.

I believe the long, hard winter can be blamed on one thing only: *As a team, we lost the clarity of our vision.*

For our entire history, we were accustomed to having a laser-focused vision that the entire church would rally around. But with the economic realities and relational strain, the vision began to leak. We found ourselves floundering with little sense of where we were heading or how we were going to get there.

It was bizarre, really, as I'm a student of vision. I've seen the power of vision, both in history books and in my own experience. I've helped hundreds of church leaders define and refine their vision. I've seen the power of a clear and compelling vision do the impossible and bring a nearly dead organization to life and strength. I'm surrounded by other leaders who also know the power of vision clarity. And yet, somehow, we couldn't pull it together. We lost our vision.

But I'm not writing this book in the middle of our five-year winter. I'm writing it as spring is beginning to emerge. There are birds chirping and green buds in the trees. It's still cold, but you can smell life in the air and occasionally feel a warm breeze across your face. Spring is always the most welcome after an extremely difficult winter. And right now, spring has never been more welcome.

I could wait awhile longer to write this book, until spring is in full bloom and there is little evidence of the winter behind us. But I'm afraid if I did that, I wouldn't remember the depths of the winter. There are enough books written on the successes of vision or the strength of a ministry strategy. Those books are fine, but my purpose is to connect you to the depths of our pain, and show you our journey out of a long winter. My purpose is also to show you the strength of finding clarity in your vision—and the process we went through to get there.

This is my fifth book, so I should have this figured out. But I have to say, I'm a bit nervous about this one. I'm telling a part of the Granger story, and so I want to get it right. Accident investigators will tell you that eyewitness accounts recorded immediately after an incident can vary wildly from person to person who all watched the same thing happen. So I have no doubt that other peoples' version of the story would differ some from mine. However, I've purposed to be as accurate as possible, drawing from my recollection and records as a member and pastor at the church for nearly two decades.

I don't want to misrepresent anyone or any part of the story. I realize that by using names, I risk giving people attention they might not desire. I also realize there are hundreds of people who are part of the story whose names do not appear. I do not want to diminish anyone's part.

But I believe I must push past my discomfort to tell the story, because it is a story of a movement of an amazing work of God in an unlikely place. I will tell you elements of our five-year winter, but I will also tell you about the amazing early days of spring. You will read about the fogginess of an unclear vision—and the crystal clear focus that vision clarity can bring.

This is the behind-the-scenes commentary of a church that grew from nothing to be labeled as one of the most innovative churches in the country—and then got stuck. You will feel our angst, but you will also smile as we celebrate significant moments along the way. You will read about the pain, the relational strain, the unbelievable mountain-top experiences, the struggle and the process that brought us to the decision of discovering a new vision that would redefine our church.

I have written this in three distinct sections, because I realize every reader will have different interests:

> **Part One – The Story.** I might be wrong, but I think everyone enjoys a good story. And I have attempted to tell you everything that is relevant, from the highest highs to the deepest lows.
>
> **Part Two – The Process.** This is for those who lead churches or organizations who are interested in the specific process we went through to discover our vision. I will also unpack the essence of the vision that is driving us into the future.
>
> **Part Three – The Tools.** If you are an organizer or systems-thinker, then this section will be like opening a present on Christmas morning. Every tool that we used is included in this section for you to copy or customize.

As we begin, I should introduce you to two misunderstood and polarizing labels. There are attractional churches. And there are missional churches. We are told you can't be both. It is possible that someone told you about our vision journey, and said, "Granger is no longer *attractional*. They have become a *missional* church." This is not true. At least not entirely.

It is taught that most churches are catering to a consumerist culture and are thus *Attractional* (used like a Christian cuss word). And, we are told, only a few churches are *Missional*. These are the good churches that are following the way of Jesus. But stick with me, because I don't think it's that clearly delineated. As I tell our story, it is my goal to define these terms, to show you why it is important you understand them and to tell you the story of one church's journey through *attractional* and *missional* to understand why it should not be an either/or argument.

The secret lies in the **AND**. It was our discovery of the **AND** that is now giving us the fuel to propel us forward with more strength and clarity than I can ever recall.

But I'm getting ahead of myself. To understand the story, we must start 25 years ago.

PART ONE: THE STORY

CHAPTER 1

THE BIRTH

The year was 1986. Mark & Sheila Beeson had been serving churches in Indiana for 15 years, being moved from location to location at the pleasure of the leaders of the United Methodist Church. They would arrive at a church that was on life support and immediately begin talking about Jesus, infusing the people with vision and building a vibrant ministry. The church would grow like crazy, hundreds would give their lives to Christ and then three or four years later, they would be moved to another church in another town, far away.

They would look over their shoulders and watch the denomination bring in another pastor who had wildly different beliefs and values; and many times they would sadly watch the church wither back to barely-alive status. This happened time and again, and it killed them.

Mark had grown up going to church every week but had a life-changing experience where he met Jesus while attending summer camp as a young teen. He saw the difference between being a life-long church member and making a decision to follow Jesus. He and Sheila both longed to serve in a place where they could see lasting impact. They wanted so deeply to build a church for people who were far from God. They wanted to build a team of leaders who had a passion to reach the community, not just host potlucks and offer bake sales. They just couldn't figure out a way to do that by rotating in and out of existing churches every few years.

So Mark began to petition the United Methodist officials: "Let me start a new church." He was told, "No Way!" more times than he could recount. So many reasons were given: "It isn't the right time." "New churches aren't needed." "You aren't the right kind of leader to start a church." But he kept asking.

One day he even went to the home of the District Superintendent in the middle of the night and put plastic forks all over the lawn, along with signs that said "Send Me!", "I'm Your Man!", and "Let Me Start a Church for You!"

It worked.

Whether it was because of his persuasive skills or because they just wanted him to go away and leave them alone—he was given permission to start a church.

But 1986 was not a good time to be starting a church in America. Mistrust of pastors and religious leaders was at an all-time high. Jimmy Swaggart, an international televangelist, had been caught with a prostitute (which he only admitted after the evidence was insurmountable). When it happened a second time, he said, "The Lord told me it's none of your business." Not a great way to build trust.

Around the same time, Jim & Tammy Faye Bakker were in the headlines every day for years as they came under fire for "financial irregularities." This included embezzling more than $3 million, selling memberships for property that didn't exist and paying off a church secretary who had accused Jim and another minister of rape. Jim eventually ended up in prison.

No, not a good time to be starting a church. Especially when you are 33 years old with big hair and plan to meet in a movie theater. In 1986, no one in our town had ever heard of church in a movie theater. That sounded too much like a Jim Bakker stunt. No, thank you.

But Mark and Sheila knew God wanted them to start a church, and that is exactly what they did. They had been told about a bedroom community in Indiana between the cities of Elkhart, South Bend and Mishawaka—two miles from the Michigan state line. The town was called Granger, which they would later find out wasn't really a town. It was just a zip code, but 46530 was predicted to be one of the highest growth areas in the state in the coming years. That prediction seemed ridiculous when they visited for the first time. They drove around for a couple hours and found nothing but farmland. They went back home disappointed.

But they didn't give up. They visited again and found some isolated subdivisions scattered between fields of corn and soybeans. As they drove around the winding streets through several neighborhoods, God broke their hearts for the people inside these brand new homes—people whom they had never met. Past all the manicured lawns and shiny cars and brick facades, they knew people were dealing with loneliness, divorce, addictions and spiritual brokenness. They began praying, asking God to build a church in Granger that would reach people who needed a Savior.

In July of 1986, Mark and Sheila Beeson moved with their three small children, ages two, four and five, to a city where they had never lived and had no friends. After six months of talking to everyone who would listen and hosting a Bible study in their home, they launched the first Sunday service on December 7, 1986. To their delight, more than 200 people attended that very first day, and Granger Community Church was born.

CHAPTER 2

THE EARLY YEARS

A one-word description of the early years might be "extreme." There were extreme highs and extreme lows. There was excitement and a fair bit of misery. Along with high levels of celebration, there were also deep seasons of pain.

One of those times was in the early 1990s when it was looking like we would be acquiring 45 acres of land on the corner of Elm and State Road 23. Vision was cast, money was raised and expectations were high. We even paid an architect several thousand dollars to develop a master plan and build a model, only to suffer disappointment later as the property slipped through our fingers.

Another time there was a terrible season of intense relational pain as the church hit 300 people and about six years old. Several of Mark and Sheila's closest friends left the church in protest. Accusations were flying, staff quit, board members resigned and many tithing families left the church. For years we would refer back to this incident as *The Train Wreck*. It was a devastating time at Granger. There were real questions about whether the church could even continue.

A few weeks later, Mark was at a conference at Willow Creek and waited in line to talk to Bill Hybels after the session. Before he could even get any words out, he broke down weeping as Bill held him and Sheila. It took a few minutes to get the story out, then Bill gave Mark some advice that would help him chart a course toward healing. He said, "You can't defend yourself. Just keep doing what you're doing, and in the next two years, everyone will know the truth."

It was the hardest thing they had ever done, but they kept just putting one foot in front of the other. And they began rebuilding the church. Rob Wegner had been hired just a few months prior to *The Train Wreck*, and was the one remaining staff member. With Rob on the team, Mark started rebuilding the staff with men and women who would help bring healing to the church. At the same time, God was preparing me for a conversation I would have with Mark that would change the course of my life.

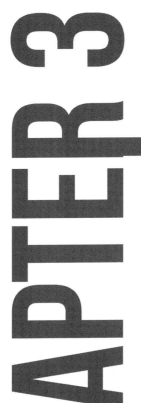

CHAPTER 3

MY FIRST VISIT

I didn't know it at the time, but my first visit to Granger was just three weeks after *The Train Wreck* had occurred. A friend of mine was being interviewed by Granger to become the worship leader, and so I visited with him on a Sunday morning in early 1993. I can still recall my feelings as I experienced a Granger service for the first time.

It's important for you to know I wasn't new to the church world. I grew up going to church every week; I attended a private Christian school at our church; and I attended Bible studies, AWANA, bus ministry, summer camp and more. Then after graduation, I joined Life Action Ministries and traveled the country working in churches. By the time I was 27, I had worked in more than 1,000 churches all over the United States and Canada. Some people could say they never missed a Sunday going to church. I can honestly say that from the time I was in second grade until I was 27, I rarely missed a *day* being in church. I was Mr. Church Guy.

But in 1993, as I sat in my first Granger service, it was like I was in church for the very first time. I had never been to a church that was so missional. That's not the word I would have used at the time. I would have said I had never been to a church so focused on reaching people far from God. I met people before and after the service who weren't your typical church-going type. There were businessmen and women who didn't normally go to church who were just checking it out. There were single parents, college students, and even a few gray-haired folks. They didn't carry their Bibles or know the words to the songs. But being in a movie theater made it comfortable for them, and you could see them leaning in and listening to every word.

Before the service, I was introduced to many people who had just made a decision to follow Jesus. They were excited about their faith. They didn't know all the right Christian words to use, and sometimes a cuss word would slip in, but they were taking their first steps. I would meet others who were first- or second-time guests. Everyone seemed excited to be there. There was a contagious buzz in the air.

For the first time ever, I was experiencing a body of believers who were *sent*. Like missionaries, they had come into a culture, studied the customs and behaviors of the people and had found the right language and way to move people toward a life in Jesus.

For many months, I sat in the services and listened to the way the gospel was being communicated. I was astonished how I could come away with such a strong sense that God was pleased, and yet none of the same words or methods were being used that I had grown up with. I looked for theological problems, but could find none. I was being forced to reevaluate many of my own assumptions and found that many of them were based on traditions and not on Scripture.

I was experiencing a missional move of God in suburban Granger. This church was accomplishing what I hadn't seen 1,000 other churches be able to do. They had come in as missionaries, studied the culture, learned the language, and sacrificed their own likes and dislikes and traditions. As a result, there were hundreds of people beginning to learn the ways of Jesus.

CHAPTER 4

JOINING THE TEAM

In April of 1994, I sat down in a sandwich shop with Mark Beeson in Anderson, Indiana. He asked me what I wanted to do with my life. He knew I was in a season of transition and was planning to leave my role at Life Action Ministries. I told him it was my goal to find a vision and a leader I could believe in and use my administrative and leadership abilities to put feet to that vision. Mark nearly erupted with enthusiasm on the spot. Still reeling from the pain of *The Train Wreck* and having spent months in intense prayer asking God to bring the right team, he was overwhelmed with emotion by my response. I can only explain his reaction by saying it looked like a volcano had just gone off, and he quickly got up and walked away from the table.

I asked the two people sitting with us what had just happened. They said, "You may be an answer to one of Mark's prayers." Within a few months, I was being interviewed for a pastoral role on the team.

The decision to hire me did not come easy. Mark was confronted by two charter families who eventually left the church in protest over the decision to hire me. They did not agree with the timing, position or funding. This was especially difficult because *The Train Wreck* had just happened 15 months earlier. These were two families who, unlike many of their friends, stayed with Mark through the turmoil of that mess. Yet now, they were leaving over a staffing decision that Mark believed would free the church up for significant growth.

On my end, just about every significant friend and spiritual leader in my life told me I would be wrong to join the Granger staff. Faith and I prayed and agonized over that decision because we were 100% sure we were heading the right direction but confused that we were receiving very little confirmation from those around us.

I specifically remember a conversation with Nancy Leigh DeMoss just before we made the transition to the staff. She was sincerely confused by our decision to leave a national ministry to join a small, 350-person local church that didn't even have a building. I said, "Nancy, I truly believe this church has the opportunity and possibility to have a world-wide impact in the coming years."

And I did believe that. It's because I didn't think of it as joining a church staff. I thought of it as becoming a missionary. I was joining a team that was being Jesus in the community we were serving, and we were totally focused on doing that in ever-increasing effectiveness. And once we figured it out, we were going to start helping churches all over the country and world do the same in their own culture.

On September 20, 1994, I showed up for my first day of "work" as a missionary at the place we called Granger Community Church. And that's when the ride began.

CHAPTER 5

THE HONEYMOON YEARS

The next 10 years were un-flippin-believable. By our 20th anniversary, we had never seen a year of losses. Every year there were more people attending than the year before. Every year there was more money in the offerings than ever before to invest in ministry.

We bought land, added services, built buildings, hired staff and expanded ministry. There were thousands of people who decided to follow Jesus and make radical life changes to adjust their life. Every year we baptized more people than any of us had ever seen baptized in a single service. And then the next year there would be even more.

One of my primary roles over the years has been staff and infrastructure, so I focused much of my time on finding the right staff and setting them up for success. We began to see people join the team with unbelievable giftedness like Kem Meyer, Tony Morgan, Dave Moore, Isaac Hunter, Mike Adkins, Mark Waltz,

Melanie Rosander and dozens more. These weren't *yes men* who had signed up to salute us when we walked down the hallway. No, these were high capacity, missional-minded creative geniuses who were wholeheartedly committed to the vision of helping every man, woman and child take their next step toward Jesus.

And the church grew like crazy.

Being wired like missionaries, and wanting to help other church leaders think like missionaries, we began hosting conferences in 1998. There were 83 leaders who showed up at our first *Building A Prevailing Church* conference. Soon after, we launched WiredChurches.com and began resourcing leaders through workshops, *Innovate* conferences, books, podcasts and more. Our philosophy was simple: If we tried something that succeeded *or* failed, we needed to pass that learning on to other church leaders.

By 2000, the church began gaining national recognition. We didn't ask for it or want it, but we began showing up on various church lists like the fastest-growing, the healthiest, the most innovative and the most influential. In 2001, Rick Warren told a publication that we were the "best example of a purpose-driven church in the country."

In 2002, I began writing the *Simply Strategic* series of books with Tony Morgan. Mark Waltz followed up a few years later with *First Impressions* and *Lasting Impressions*. Upon publication, these five titles became critical handbooks for tens of thousands of pastors and leaders who were interested in the "under the hood" practices of church leadership. More than a dozen seminaries notified us they were using one or more of these books as required reading.

And the church continued to grow. We had a difficult time keeping up with the crowds. We'd be running out of seats, so we'd start a new service. Just a few weeks later, it would fill up and we'd have the same problem again. We had terrible parking problems, so we built a new parking lot. In less than a year, it was full. We doubled our children's center believing it would give us growth for years. In just a few months, many rooms were already over-flowing.

It was an amazing run of ministry. Like Joseph in the Old Testament, it seemed like God granted success to everything we put our hands on. John Maxwell talks about momentum and calls it *The Big Mo*. We had *The Big Mo* for so many years, we couldn't picture life without it. Our leadership team communicated like a well oiled machine. Mark Beeson would often describe the difference between his role and mine as being "two wings of the same bird." He would teach and cast vision; I would work on strategy and run the church. We were completely opposite in personality and leadership style and yet were in perfect sync on values and major decisions.

Everything was going amazingly well. That is, until Tuesday, October 12, 2004.

CHAPTER 6

THE BIG JOLT

I was sitting in my office when a soft knock came at the door. It was a woman who had been in the church since the earliest days. She was an amazing leader who had grown in her faith and raised her daughter at the church. She and her husband were among the most loved people at Granger and two of my dearest friends.

Six years prior to this October day, we had invited her to join our staff, followed soon by an invitation to serve with us on the senior leadership team. Just two years before this knock, she had become one of our pastors. This was a woman I had grown to love and admire, and I never imagined doing ministry at Granger without her.

But the look on her face would change everything. She was coming to tell me that she had messed up. She had become inappropriately entangled with a man on her staff—a man who was also married. His wife had found out about it and given her an ultimatum to talk to me or be exposed.

What we uncovered in emails during the next several days showed us the affair was deeper than any of us could imagine. She instantly resigned and cleaned out her office. She and her husband left the church never to return. The man who was involved was fired, and within weeks, we also lost our worship leader, who was a close relative of hers.

This rocked our world. It threw us off our game. It put the brakes on our momentum. I can't find words to explain how devastating this was for our team.

It wasn't the moral failure that threw us off balance. We had weathered such things before. Just two years before, another staff member had been caught involved in immoral activity. And before that, we let a staff member quietly resign who was using church computers to conduct promiscuous activities with others online.

But there was something about this situation that shook us to our core, and Mark and I got out of sync. In the days that followed, he made some decisions that I had a hard time supporting, and I made some decisions that caused him to lose trust in me. The pace of ministry was so fast that we never took the time to stop and talk. With trips, vacations and the tyranny of the urgent, we kept missing each other. For weeks following *The Big Jolt*, I was working 14- to 16-hour days making decisions, counseling staff and church members through their pain and planning services (because even though we had lost the core of our creative arts team, Sunday still came every weekend).

I can clearly remember during this season getting out of bed in the middle of the night and putting on a jacket for a walk around the neighborhood to clear my head. I was mad. I was stressed. I was hurting because I felt such deep loss at losing two very close friends. I was yelling at God and asking Him why I had to be a leader at a time like this. I didn't know what to do and felt like I was getting hit from every side. It was more than I could bear. I eventually came back to the house and cried myself to sleep.

That event in October 2004, and the decisions we made in the following days, led us into a dark season as a church. Little did we know, the darkness would last nearly five years.

CHAPTER 7

THE FUNK

Have you ever been in a *Funk*, where it feels like you are walking through mud with every footstep just to get to the next place? Sometimes a personal *Funk* might begin as a result of a traumatic incident, the loss of friends, a chemical imbalance, or a lack of purpose. Sometimes you can't even figure out the reason; you just know that every step is hard, every conversation seems laced with multiple agendas and it's impossible to get even the simplest tasks accomplished.

In the days following *The Big Jolt*, we just kept moving forward—planning services, making decisions, hiring staff. But in hindsight, I can see that we were mired in a quicksand of hurt and confusion. We were in a season of *Funk* and needed help. We didn't know it at the time, but we'd lost a clear and compelling vision. We were dealing with our own personal hurts that stripped us of our ability to lead the church with strength.

About six years prior, during *The Honeymoon*, we had set out with an ambitious 10-year vision that made everyone suck air as they tried to get their minds around the magnitude of what we thought God could accomplish through us. That vision provided wind in our sails for years. But by 2006, we had seen most of it accomplished, and we began wondering, "What is next?" People were taking steps to follow Jesus and get baptized by the hundreds, and we celebrated that. But it didn't have the sense of "movement" and "revolution" as in the early days. Rather than, "No way! Look what God did!", the response became, "Of course. That's what happens here. Been there, done that."

Good things continued to happen in the season of *The Funk*. We launched a multi-site location; we continued to train pastors and start hundreds of churches in southern India; we made tremendous strides in our community center in downtown South Bend; and we saw marriages healed and hundreds give their lives to Jesus. But we just weren't firing on all cylinders. There was a growing awareness that something wasn't right.

During the first couple years of *The Funk* the church continued to grow. But we had lost *The Big Mo*. We were riding the wave of the previous 10 years, so it was awhile before we noticed. But eventually the growth slowed. And then it stopped. And then decline set in.

And it killed us.

We kept trying stuff that would have some degree of success, but things were unclear. It was like running toward a finish line through a dense fog and trying to course-correct without being able to see past your nose. We'd launch an initiative that we were sure would get us back on track. It would start with a bang but then fizzle out after awhile. So we'd try something else. And then something else. But we weren't being driven *toward* a new vision. We were being driven *away* from failure.

During the season of *The Funk*, some of our relationships got sideways. We spent more and more time in our senior team meetings arguing over what was broke and how to fix it, and we let it damage some of our friendships. When things are great, you don't have to spend much time evaluating ("It must be working, right?"). But when you are in the season of *The Funk* and the numbers are decreasing and you can't figure out how to get out of it, you tend to blame people and cancel programs. And sometimes we blamed the wrong people and canceled the wrong programs.

We sat through agonizing meetings trying to figure out the problem. We prayed. We cried. We argued. We blamed ourselves. We blamed the economy. We blamed the weather. We blamed the congregation and their lack of an evangelistic fervor. We blamed our location. We blamed our programming. We blamed our own relational deficiencies. Sometimes, we even blamed each other.

So we started changing stuff. We changed personnel. We changed service times. We added locations. We took surveys. We discontinued entire ministries. We made services longer. We made services shorter. We tried using more pop culture—then less pop culture. We made services more experiential. We tried offering felt need topics more. We tried going deeper.

Nothing was working.

Truthfully, the worst part of *The Funk* was my relationship with Mark Beeson. After more than a decade of being in perfect sync, our relationship had spiraled down to a point of terrible pain and dysfunction. For the first time in our history together, Mark would reverse some of my decisions, which caused me to lose my confidence as a leader. Conversely, Mark felt like I didn't value him as a person or a leader, which brought insecurity and caused him to stop leading with strength. Our relational troubles, though mostly hidden, had a devastating impact on our ability to lead and thus hurt the entire church.

Sometimes, in a season of *Funk*, you will think about leaving. I know I did. In February 2008, I was experiencing the most difficult days since joining the team at Granger, struggling to work through daily tension with Mark that neither one of us could figure out how to fix. I wasn't even sure he wanted to work with me any more. On top of all that, it was 10 degrees below zero with more than two feet of snow on the ground, and I was tired of winter. And the call I received was from a wonderful church in sunny Phoenix, Arizona. I'll be honest–I thought about leaving.

Others did leave. Sometimes when the team is losing, people will take their bat and ball and decide to play on someone else's team—a team that is winning more games, a team that still has *The Big Mo*. Those were hard discussions, but I understood. Everyone needs to believe they are making a difference.

We also experienced leaders who began to check out mentally. Some who had a clear sense of their wiring and purpose began to find their fulfillment doing side jobs, consulting gigs, or other projects outside the church. This was understandable but especially frustrating to Mark. He felt like some were more interested in building their side-job resume of success than in accepting the responsibility of making Granger strong again. But most stayed on the team, almost like they were waiting for *The Big Mo* to return and our vision to be big enough to capture their imagination once again.

CHAPTER 8

A LEADER'S PERSPECTIVE

(BY MARK BEESON)

I asked Mark Beeson to write out his thoughts on our dark season. Here is how he described that season in his own words:

Your strengths are often your weaknesses, too. I know that, but when I failed to give heed to the cautions I've built into my self-leadership process, I failed my team. The consequence was a season of discord and strife that hurt our team for years, and it's my own fault. Whatever anyone else said or did, I failed to see the downside of overindulging my upside.

What's my upside?

I love team. I love identifying, recruiting and training great people so they can achieve greater success. I'm happiest when I can lead someone to help his or her team achieve mission success. I love that. There's nothing quite like delegating responsibility and entrusting mission-minded leaders with the authority to help their teammates win.

But delegation isn't the same thing as abdication, and when mission drift pulls a team off course, a leader who has not only delegated but has also abdicated has no easy way to correct and redirect the team.

If you've abdicated, how can you help?

That's what I did. It was the worst leadership action of my life. Oh, my intentions were good, but the road to hell is paved with good intentions, right? I intended to give people enough room to soar, but I failed to deliver ongoing collaborative vision, encouragement and honest feedback. I wanted to communicate trust, but I failed to connect, and we lost synergy. I gave so much space that some of the great leaders on my team felt disconnected. I wanted my team to feel like they were cut free to do great things, but some of them felt cut off, as if I no longer cared about what they did, how they did it or who they became in the process.

Mission drift led to discord. Discord, as it always does, caused people to look for a leader willing to chart a clear course, rally the troops to a renewed vision and lead the charge toward the preferred future. I had that responsibility, but I was so focused on entrusting others with power and delegating authority that I failed to recognize my ongoing place in that process. I had delegated on purpose, but when mission success required my leadership, I didn't know how to engage my team.

I had confused delegation with abdication and feared my leadership would communicate a lack of trust. I worried that if I led with vision and strength, after delegating so much power and responsibility to such capable leaders, my teammates would think I had no confidence in them. That paralyzed me. So I did virtually nothing. It was the worst leadership decision of my life.

I didn't understand what was happening. I didn't see what I had done. I couldn't figure it out and had no viable solution. I was in a leadership mess and didn't know what to do.

Months passed as I examined my life, talked with my wife, read the Bible and prayed.

That's when God spoke.

It wasn't long sentences. It wasn't difficult to understand.

One December morning God gave me one word: *"Lead."* That word changed my life. That word changed my leadership. As if God had flipped a toggle switch in my heart, I understood, at the depth of my being, that God's mandate was for me to lead.

So I did.

I started by telling my teammates the truth, that while I imagined I was delegating well, I had abdicated my role on the team. I confessed that I'd failed them and asked forgiveness. I told them how God had answered my prayers and surprised me with one word of direction, telling me to lead. I assured them I intended to obey God, serve them well and accomplish my assignment.

And, after such a long season of confusion, strife and team trauma, I began to lead again.

The day God broke in and intercepted my life was the day God returned our team to the path of unity and missional success.

I'll never forget it.

—**Mark Beeson**

THE RECOVERY

Several things contributed to our recovery, including Mark's experience with God on that December morning. It was not an immediate journey out of the valley, but I believe *The Funk* conclusively came to an end in early 2009 when we had to make the awful decision to lay off eight people and cut hours for 15 others. It is interesting to me, in hindsight, that our coming together as a leadership team to make the toughest decision we had ever faced was the very impetus that took us on a path toward recovery.

In January 2009, the global economic crisis was at its peak with no signs of letting up. Local unemployment topped 20 percent, and the New York Times described the counties around our church as "the white-hot center of the meltdown of the American economy." Every day I heard of someone else in our church who had lost his or her job. Trickle-down economics was working in reverse on us: A poor economy affected jobs; loss of jobs affected income; loss of income affected contributions; and lower contributions meant we couldn't pay as many staff.

We did everything we could to avoid layoffs: cutting budgets, freezing salaries, eliminating capital expenses and delaying projects. But in the end, it wasn't enough. The decision had to be made.

But in this crisis, our senior team became as unified as I had ever known. I've heard it said that a terrible tragedy will either drive a family together or tear it apart. What is true for a family is also true for an organization. This decision, as hard as it was, drove our team together. We began to operate in sync once again. We began to dream about the future. We began to, once again, ask God about His vision for Granger.

The Big Mo was beginning to return, ever so slowly at first. But you could feel it.

CHAPTER 10

A CHANGING CULTURE

As we came out of the cloudiness of *The Funk*, we were facing some difficult challenges. We realized by the middle of 2009, we could no longer do church the same way we'd always done it. Culture had changed.

I'm not a historian or anthropologist, so I will leave it to much smarter people to explain why culture has shifted so dramatically in recent years. But I have a theory. I believe that the failure of the banking industry in late 2008, and the government's inability to predict it or stop it, was the proverbial straw that broke the camel's back in the average American's trust of the institution. Since the 1960s, Americans have grown increasingly wary of anything that is organized or institutional. The Vietnam War, Watergate, Clinton's Lewinsky scandal and the lack of WMDs in Iraq obliterated our trust in government. Enron, Lehman Brothers and the BP oil disaster greatly diminished any trust we had in corporate

America. And the televangelist scandals along with the Catholic Church cover-ups of sexual abuse have stripped away America's trust of religious institutions. On top of the national scandals, just about every local newspaper in America has had headlines about pastors involved in infidelity or embezzlement. It's no wonder that churches are in the mix.

Simultaneous to these cultural changes, technology has been giving people power they never had before. They no longer need to believe the "company line" from the corporate, government or religious institution. Technology gives them access to their own "expert" with no need to come to us.

It all adds up to a highly divided American culture that is very cynical and non-trusting of anything institutional. I see very little chance that the pendulum will swing back. Today's reality is the new normal.

Our team began to talk about this in earnest during 2009. At the same time that we were asking, "What is God's vision for Granger in the next five or 10 years?", we were also becoming more aware that things were going to have to change significantly.

Back in the early days, and all the way up until 2007, we could plan a service and put out chairs, and every seat would be filled. It was easy for people to invite their friends.

By 2009, we were getting reports that it was becoming much more difficult for our congregation to invite their friends. Was it because we weren't the new kid in town any more? Was it because the novelty of a church like Granger had worn off? Was it because there were other similar churches in town? Was it because some churches starting up around us were offering "deeper" teaching?

Maybe all of those explanations were true to some degree. But bigger than all of that, we believed it was because culture was shifting. And God was doing something in our hearts preparing us to meet the challenge.

Rob Wegner and I began to talk very seriously about this in mid-2009. God was doing something inside of him that was about to wake all of us up. He came back from a personal retreat of silence and solitude with what he believed was a word from God. It was all wrapped around a 2020 vision for Granger. And it was huge. I remember as he shared it with me, I didn't know how to respond. Some of it I connected with, but some of it I didn't even understand. Here is what he presented to me in September 2009:

By 2020…
- *Plant 20,200 churches in the most unreached places of the world.*
- *Transform 2,020 communities through church-based community development initiatives and cultural catalysts.*
- *Coach 2,020 existing churches through missional moves.*
- *Launch 220 churches in America through multi-site, church-planting, or micro-church.*
- *Connect 20,200 people in our area in missional community at Granger.*
- *Coach 2,020 next step leaders in the Granger movement*
- *Transform culture by raising up 220 cultural catalysts to 'bring up there down here.' These catalysts would become our area's top 220 influencers in education, politics, health care, arts, business and faith.*

He scribbled on the bottom of his list: "Lord, show me what to do with this. This is the church I want to lead, shepherd and serve. Lord, let Granger be that church."

I was amazed, stretched, humbled, excited and scared. I felt unworthy. "God, is this your direction for Granger?" I knew it wasn't my decision alone to make. Rob shared the same list with Mark Beeson. All three of us were praying, listening, talking, thinking, learning and asking God for wisdom.

CHAPTER 11

A PARALLEL JOURNEY

I mentioned that we saw great success in India and downtown South Bend during *The Funk*, but the story would be incomplete if I didn't unpack this a bit more for you. In 2001, as the church was turning 15 years old, we began to broaden our church-wide focus on missions beyond our local neighborhoods. We began to ask, "Where does God want us to put our laser-focused energy with an unreached people group somewhere around the world?" We didn't want to be the church with a scattered approach and 50 different pins of influence on a global map. Rather, we wanted to have a deep, long-lasting impact in one location.

In early 2001, Mark Beeson, Rob Wegner and I took a trip to Germany and Albania to begin to look for possible partnerships. Rob was charged with "taking our church to the world" and invested time in other trips to remote locations like Sudan. Eventually, through a partnership with Ron Vandergriend (a Granger member) and the church-planting division of The Bible League, we landed in Tamil Nadu, the southern-most state in India.

Over the next 10 years, we partnered with The Bible League and other organizations to train hundreds of Indian pastors and start more than 1,000 churches. As of the printing of this book, there are 147,688 believers meeting in 1,133 churches led by 970 pastors trained through our network. D. Rajendran, who is now on staff with Granger and the Director of Life Mission International, leads our disciple-making efforts in India. It has truly been a move of God!

Similarly, and around the same time, a couple Granger volunteers began mentoring children living in the Monroe Circle public housing complex near downtown South Bend, Indiana. This is a neighborhood within 20 minutes of our church campus that has experienced generational poverty for decades. After a few years of helping kids, the director of a nearby food pantry asked Granger to help provide food for their ministry. Volunteers began helping with food and other small rehab jobs that the building desperately needed. Eventually, the owners of the food pantry offered to sell the building to Granger for one dollar. In January 2005, we took over the pantry and began the effort to acquire all three adjoining buildings. Through donated funds, labor, gifts "in-kind" and other community and business partnerships, the Monroe Circle Community Center* emerged. The mission of this ministry is to help each adult and each child living in that troubled community take his or her next step toward a full and meaningful life. We want to add value and help each person discover his or her worth for the purpose of developing a vibrant, safe and strong community with strong families.

---

* See MonroeCircle.com for more information.

These two experiences "out there" were happening at the same time we were experiencing *The Big Jolt, The Funk* and eventually *The Recovery*. And they were teaching us many new things about church. I'm sure this list is incomplete, but here are a few things we were learning:

- Our church-planting model in India was mostly happening through what might be called "missional communities." We were training Indian men and women (who had day jobs) to learn their culture, begin to meet the needs of their community and start a church. With no building, no staff, no budget and no land, their place of worship would start under a banyan tree or on the rooftop of a building. They wouldn't hang up a sign announcing the start of a new church; instead they would begin to have conversations with their family and friends or the person who cuts their hair or sells them fruit, and a church would begin to emerge.
- A few of these church starts turned into larger gatherings meeting in buildings, but most of them just reproduced like rabbits into more gatherings of 20 to 30 people.
- In India, we weren't employing the "come to us" model that is prevalent in the American culture. Instead we were finding ways to take Jesus into the community.
- In South Bend, we were reaching people through a Community Center model. Rather

than start with a central gathering (aka "church service") and eventually meet the needs of the community, we launched with the sole purpose of being Jesus' hands and feet to the community. It was several years before a weekly church service gathering became a part of the ministry of Monroe Circle.

- As we met needs with no agenda, we began to forge partnerships (and thus relationships) with other organizations in the greater South Bend area. Our impact multiplied when the City realized we were serious about community transformation.

So Rob's dream wasn't a list of pie-in-the-sky numbers that he pulled from his … er, head. They were based on what we had seen God do already through the people of Granger in India and South Bend. The question: Could He also do this through our campuses in Granger and Elkhart? We were already sensing that it was becoming more difficult for people to invite their friends to attend a service. Maybe we needed a parallel strategy? Maybe we needed to take our learnings from "out there" and employ them closer to home.

I wasn't sure if Rob's list was the right direction, and I wasn't sure what parts of our strategy in India and South Bend would work at our suburban campuses. But I knew God was getting ready to take us someplace we'd never been. I believed we needed to be ready for it, but as I looked at our leadership team, I didn't think it was adequate.

CHAPTER 12

A NEW LEADERSHIP TEAM

Two years before I had proposed bringing some new people onto our senior leadership team. At that time, Mark and I weren't in a good place, and I wasn't able to convince him that the shift was a good change for the church. He was right; we weren't ready. By the fall of 2009, we were in a completely different place. He and I were two wings of the same bird again, and we both knew it was time. In December, we announced to the staff that we were adding three additional leaders to our senior team. The new team would be:

Mark Beeson – senior pastor
Tim Stevens – executive pastor
Rob Wegner – pastor of life mission
Mark Waltz – pastor of connections

Kem Meyer (new) – communications director
DC Curry (new) – director of youth ministries
Jason Miller (new) – pastor of creative arts

I can't describe to you the significant change that one deci-sion brought to the church. It went way beyond my expectation. There was a diversity that I knew we needed, but I didn't know how much it was holding us back. I'm not speaking of gender diversity, even though Kem is a woman; or ethnic diversity, even though DC is African-American; or age diversity, even though DC and Jason were in their 20s at the time. It was all of that and more. These three leaders brought fresh ideas and insights. They brought unique perspective and a different kind of wisdom. They helped us get unstuck from the mire that we were in and provided an engine of ideas to propel us forward.

I was positive it would take months for us all to begin gell-ing together before we could have productive meetings. I couldn't have been more wrong. From the very first meeting, we clicked as though we had been together for years.

That was exactly the atmosphere we needed to tackle our next assignment.

CHAPTER 13

EMBARKING ON A NEW VISION

In January 2010, our senior team went away to a cabin in Michigan for our annual planning retreat. This would be the first retreat with our expanded team. We had invited Todd Wilson, a church leadership consultant and management guru, to join us. He was going to lead us for two days through a Peter Drucker strategic exercise to help give us a framework for our next steps. We were going to use that as a foundation for the final two days of planning.

While I was driving to the cabin on the first day of the retreat, I received a call from Todd. He was in our local airport but had just received notice of a family emergency. He was calling to inform me he would have to return to his home. It was less than an hour before our retreat was to begin and the primary facilitator who was driving the agenda for the first two days had just canceled. I felt bad for his emergency, but frankly, I was more concerned with what we were going to do during the next two days.

In hindsight, Todd's cancellation was a blessing straight from God. Those four days ended up being the tunnel we passed through on our way from the old Granger to the new vision to which God was calling us.

We spent several hours that first day talking about, and reaffirming our belief in, the mission of the church. *"Helping People Take Their Next Step Toward Christ … Together"* had remained unchanged since the first days of the church. And we embraced it again with new passion. We also spent several hours modifying our Core Values. We kept a few the same, threw a couple out and wrote some new ones. It was a good exercise*.

Then we turned the corner. We began to have a conversation we should have started four years earlier. We began talking about our new vision. We were all acutely aware of the need the church had to hear from their leaders on our vision. The congregation was ready. They wanted to know where we were going next.

Mark and I put our heads together for a few minutes early the second day of the retreat and decided to see what everyone was thinking individually about our vision before we had any conversation as a group. So we came together and talked briefly about the definition of vision: *Vision is a picture of a preferred future.* Then we gave the assignment: "Go find a corner of the house to be alone. Pray and write out your vision for Granger by the year 2020. You have two hours."

When everyone reconvened, we had what may have been the most unified few hours ever experienced by any leadership team on the planet. I might be exaggerating, but probably not. It was A-MA-ZING how tight our individual vision statements were before we'd ever had conversation as a group. The Spirit of God

---

* You can read these beginning on page 202.

had been working in each of us, one-by-one, for months, even years, to bring us to the place where we were all ready for the same path. And it would be a wildly different and more expansive path than any of us had been on before.

Here is just one line from each of those vision statements that we shared with each other in January 2010:

> **Jason Miller** – "Every Christ-follower at GCC will understand that obedience to Jesus Christ transforms relationships in families, work places and neighborhoods into venues for mission, effectively mobilizing 15,000 Kingdom agents in the transformation of our world."

> **Tim Stevens** – "I see a church that is leading the way for community transformation in justice (lower crime rates), education (better graduation rates), families (lower divorce rates) and education (higher literacy)."

> **DC Curry** – "We will be committed to producing environments that help people be transformed by Jesus ... not just *inspired* by Him."

> **Kem Meyer** – "We would build a place where people can mobilize anytime, anywhere, to experience faith, hope, love, kindness and training for innovation, leadership and community building."

Mark Beeson – "We will have 2,020 lay pastors who will be leading 2,020 'Essential Churches' of 20 people each by the year 2020."

Rob Wegner – "The church campus will no longer be a destination, but a hub for training, encouragement, vision-casting, corporate worship and commissioning. People who 'are' the church will have embraced the uncomfortable reality that most spiritual formation and transformation MUST happen and can only happen at home, at work and on mission in the world while serving others, especially the poor and the lost."

Mark Waltz – "We will be influencing the culture's art with innovation, training and forums wherein the church leads, shapes and celebrates God's beauty and Gospel message."

Those are just snippets of what we wrote, but they give you an idea of the common themes across all of them. Each of us read our vision aloud and had a few minutes to share our heart about where we believed God might be taking the church. There were similarities that began to emerge. The next season would not be measured primarily by attendance or baptisms but by impact in and through our community. This vision was going to take more than a few paid staff members leading. It was going to require every follower of Jesus discovering their God-given missional impulses and getting in the game.

The vision was huge. We were beginning to turn the corner. But the decision we made next might surprise you.

KEM MEYER: COMMUNICATIONS DIRECTOR

I had been a member of the senior team for a whopping month when we went to the cabin for our planning retreat. Let that sink in. One month. I wasn't approaching anything about this week with familiarity or self-assurance. My eyes were as big as saucers. And, my whole plan going into the week was to survive with an entry-level training strategy. You know, figure out the basics—when do I speak up, when do I shut up and various drills of that nature. When I heard our assignment at the start of the second morning, I about had a heart attack. I was still trying to figure out what I was even doing in the room, and my first task was to draft a 10-year vision for Granger?

If you could have only seen the thoughts flooding my head in the first few minutes: "I'm in over my head. I don't know what I'm doing. Can't we please work on this as a group? How about I just get caught up on email and provide feedback when you're done? This will be my first and last retreat, won't it? I'm a punk. What if my version doesn't fit?" The pressure was tremendous. I know. Joe Cool. That's me.

But those thoughts didn't last long, and I started to hear an inner voice stronger than my own: "I love you, Kem, but you're going bonkers right now. Reality check: These leaders know what they're getting into with you and so do I. Where's the trust? Where's the love? Come on, now. Take a deep breath and just start writing what I've put on your heart." Read: Quit being a big cry baby, and do the job you've been given.

My heart was still racing, but I found my corner, opened my laptop, emailed my husband asking him to pray for us and went to work. Tim's version says two hours, but I remember it more like three minutes. That's how fast the time flew.

We came back together and starting going around the room, each person reading his or her own vision draft out loud. I was stunned at the unity woven into seven individual perspectives. I wanted to cry, but it would have been too cliché. It was a faith-building moment. My heart was still racing, but then it was for completely different reasons.

CHAPTER 14

SHELVING THE VISION

We easily could have taken our seven individual vision statements and written a combined document by the end of that retreat. We could have driven back to Granger and presented the new vision to the congregation. We were that unified as a team.

But we took some time to consider carefully what we were going to do next. This was the third time since the beginning of the church that such a conversation was taking place. In 1994, the church was eight years old with around 400 people attending when Mark traveled to Korea as part of a doctoral studies program. On that trip, he went up a Prayer Mountain and believed God gave him a clear vision of what the church should be about in the coming years. He believed that God was asking Granger to love and care for 2,000 people by the year 2000. I still remember the service when he shared that vision with the church for the first time. There was an audible gasp from the audience—then applause. No one had ever seen or heard of a church that large in our area. It felt like a God-sized dream.

By 1999, we were consistently averaging over 1,800 and growing quickly toward 2,000. It was time for a new vision. This time, however, God didn't give the vision to Mark. Instead, he gave it to the leaders. We spent about 15 months in a process with a group of staff and volunteer leaders developing the 2010 vision. It was much more detailed this time—with metrics and goals in seven different categories.

If the 1994 vision was Moses coming off the mountain with a word from God, then the 1999 vision process was the entire leadership team doing the same thing. There was nothing wrong with the Moses-method. But having the entire leadership team involved in the formation of the vision brought a whole new power to the process.

In 2010, we had a decision to make. Should we choose the 1994 "Moses" model? Or should we choose the 1999 "Team" model? We decided on neither. Instead, we spent time developing a 2010 "Crowd-Sourced" model. We believed it was crucial to pull the entire congregation into the process. Not just the pastors. Not just the key leaders. But every single person in the church.

We realized, though, to do this right and genuinely involve every person in the church, it would take as long as a year. That meant another year without a clear vision to move forward.

That was a difficult decision, because we so desperately needed an infusion of momentum. Many of our leaders were just waiting for us to point the way. Everyone was primed for new direction. But I believe it was exactly the right decision for several very important reasons:

1. Mark Beeson would be taking a sabbatical later in the year and be gone for three months. It didn't make sense to release our vision right before he departed.

2. We believed the long-term strength of having the ownership of the entire church was going to offset the short-term loss of waiting a year.

3. We had a sense that this new vision was going to revolve significantly around the people of the church. It wasn't going to be about new programs or services or sites to serve them. It was going to be about resourcing them to become active in the world. And for this reason, this vision needed to come from them.

4. We had gone through three years of introducing new direction from our senior leaders, only to see it fizzle out over time. This happened again and again. If this new vision was going to have staying power, it needed to come from the people.

It turns out there was another reason to wait that we didn't know at the time. God had much to teach us about our journey as a church. And he did so in a very unexpected way—through an Australian named Alan Hirsch.

CHAPTER 15

FUTURE TRAVELERS

We came home from our planning retreat, and Rob began to petition me about a new learning environment with a small group of leaders called *Future Travelers**. I didn't know what it was, and I wasn't interested. Rob continued learning more about it and found out it consisted of a group of leaders from 10 large churches who were asking some of the same questions we were asking. Rob was convinced that we needed to get involved. He believed we would learn so much by just being in the same room as these other leaders.

But I was extremely busy and didn't have time to add a four-day gathering to my plate twice each year. Plus there was going to be some cost involved, and money was one thing we couldn't afford to waste. I tried to convince Rob to go by himself, but he

---

* Learn more about Future Travelers at Missional.com

inquired and found out it was all or nothing. Either Mark, Rob and I all had to commit, or none of us could participate.

Rob finally convinced me, but we knew there was no way we were going to convince Mark without more information. So we finally got them to agree to let Rob and I attend the first function in Austin, Texas, by ourselves. Then we could decide if Granger was in or out after that. If Rob and I felt like it would bring value to the church, then we'd go back and convince Mark to attend the next gathering.

But honestly, at that point I was only going to Austin to be a support to Rob. I knew it was important to him and therefore it was worth it to me. I also place a great deal of trust in Rob and his ability to sense where God is at work. So I thought, "Maybe there is something here for us to learn." But I really didn't want to go.

One reason for my attitude was my dislike for academic "experts" who had built nothing, done nothing and led no one. That was my perception of this Alan Hirsch guy (although I later found out I was wrong). If I was going to learn from someone, it was going to be from a practitioner, not a theorist.

Even though I had a closed mind, I began reading Alan Hirsch's book on the airplane on the way to Austin. It was called, *The Forgotten Ways**, and is a book about rediscovering the missional origin of the Church. The more I read, the more I hung on every word. God began to penetrate my closed mind, reach my heart and speak to me as clearly as he ever had.

But as I read, I was struggling with one word: "Missional."

---

* Alan Hirsch, *The Forgotten Ways* (Grand Rapids, MI: Brazos Press, 2006).

CHAPTER 16

MISSIONAL SCHMISSIONAL

I've been in ministry for more than 25 years now, and I've seen lots of fads come and go. Every few years, we've been told there is a new model or philosophy or way of thinking that we should build our church around. A few examples:

- Bus Ministry (oh yeah, I'm really that old)
- Small groups
- Meta-Model
- Purpose-Driven
- Next generation or Gen X ministry
- Post-Modern or Post-Christian
- Emergent or Emerging
- Seeker-sensitive or Seeker-driven
- Third Place
- Multi-site

Each new model tells us why the way we are doing church isn't working or isn't good enough. We are told how all the previous model were fads and the newest one is going to replace all of them. We are told we need to change everything, go back to the drawing board and do something different—because everything we've done in the past was misguided, ineffective and possibly even sinful.

The most recent example? *Missional.* These days, it seems like every conference, leader, blog and interview is talking about how missional is the bomb and attractional is yesterday.

Do you ever hear leaders talk about missional-this or missional-that and want to say "Missional Schmissional"? I know I do. I hear a supposed missional expert make over-stated points about how most churches these days are inward focused and consumer-centric and they don't care whether people around them are going to hell, and then they say, "Oh by the way, that's called 'Attractional' which is synonymous with evil." And then they tell you, "Missional is the answer!", and I want to say, "Missional schmissional."

The exaggerated, over-stated arguments cause me at times to want to throw out the entire conversation. I have a very good friend who I've known for decades who recently read a popular missional book. His eyes were opened to the evils of the institutional church (insert sarcasm here). He learned how church buildings, pastors and worship leaders are all unbiblical. So my friend left his church. He's not doing "house church," nor is he doing "missional life" with anyone—he's just done with church. I walked away from my friend and wanted to say, "Missional schmissional."

I have a friend at a church that was growing by leaps and bounds in the 1990s. In a fairly small community, they had as many as 3,500 people attending every weekend, and they hosted conferences and told people how to grow their church. But then, they stopped growing. For a while they were silent. They stopped doing conferences; they just kind of fell off the radar. Before long, however, they began writing books and hosting conferences and telling people they changed their mind. "Church growth is actually bad!" they proclaimed. It was like they could no longer produce the results by which they measured success, so they just moved the target. They started saying, "Oh, it's not the quantity. It's the quality." They started saying, "It's all about missional impact, and that's really hard to track, so just trust us, we are successful at this." When I heard that, I wanted to say, "Missional schmissional."

About 10 years ago, I attended a conference that was all about the emerging church, with many speakers using the words "missional" and "emerging" interchangeably. At the conference, I saw some people dancing in the aisles, others running rakes through sand and still others drawing hideous pictures on canvas during the message. Some people in the audience would just stand up and start talking to the crowd. I got weirded out! And I wanted to say, "If this is missional, then missional schmissional."

I hear the over-generalizations about attractional and I think, "I've never seen that church." I don't know of one pastor anywhere who doesn't care about the people in his or her community. It seems every attractional church pastor is painted as selfish, consumer-focused and interested only in money and big buildings. "They all care more about numbers than people," we are told. I don't know of a pastor like that. I don't know of a church that doesn't want people to live missionally in their everyday lives. I don't know of a church that is just about the weekend experience and does nothing else to serve people. So when I hear the attractional church or pastor described that way and missional as the answer, I want to say, "Missional schmissional."

So you can imagine when I'm first reading Alan's book about "missional churches," I'm mostly rolling my eyes. I'm expecting the same "my way or the highway" attitude I've heard from others. But then I see that Alan has the same concern I do. He said, "It has become increasingly difficult to open a ministry book or attend a church conference and not be accosted by the word missional. A quick search on Google uncovers the presence of "missional communities," "missional leaders," "missional worship," even "missional seating," and "missional coffee." Today, everyone wants to be missional."*

The first time I recall seeing the words "missional" and "attractional" used together was in 2005 when Tony Morgan and I wrote a book called *Simply Strategic Growth*. Leonard Sweet, an author, professor and strategic thinker, was nice enough to offer an endorsement for the back cover. He wrote: "Don't let the attractional language fool you. This book is really about 'missional' Christianity and meeting the culture where it's at, not where you wish it were." I remember talking to Tony and saying, "What the heck does that mean?"

I didn't know it at the time, but the "attractional" label was beginning to emerge to describe the "come and see" model of ministry. And often, it was being used as a term of derision to describe the model of church to which I had given my life! Once I figured that out, I didn't like it one bit. I didn't like the implication that there was something wrong with creating a weekend church service that was so compelling and so relevant that people invited their friends to come with them! I didn't like it when people

---

* ChristianityToday.com, *Defining Missional*, December 12, 2008, http://www.christianitytoday.com/le/communitylife /evangelism/17.20.html?gclid=COrBvrjsn6sCFQ1b7Aodd BwThQ&start=1

suggested that it was futile to talk about topics that were so close to people's hearts that it was easy for them to walk into a church to get help with their marriage or money or loneliness. And by doing so, we'd have an opportunity to introduce them to Jesus.

Hearing a growing voice of Christian leaders label my church as attractional and simultaneously call it ineffective, unbiblical or both kind of felt like someone had just said my wife is ugly.

CHAPTER 17

ATTRACTIONAL SCHMACTIONAL

But, if I'm gut-level honest, sometimes I see their point (no, not about my gorgeous wife). I've been doing this "come and see" model of church for nearly two decades now. And sometimes I get tired of it and want to say, "Attractional schmactional."

Sometimes I get tired of the performance. Sometimes the "show" wears me out. I see people come for a while, get on fire and get involved, and then a couple years later they are just gone. They fade away. It no longer works for them.

Sometimes it feels like every week has to be better than the week before. The amazing series that we did last month or last year is gone all too quickly, and the only lasting impact is that now we have to do better on the next one. Sometimes that makes me want to say, "Attractional schmactional."

It's like the actor who is only as good as his most recent movie. He may have been in a blockbuster a couple years ago that made millions of dollars—but if he hasn't been in anything lately, he is deemed a failure. If our messages aren't ever-better, if our artistry and videos and dramas and graphic designs and series creativity and building design and coffee flavors aren't better than last week, then we are stagnant. We are yesterday's news. And it gets old.

Why? Because we are only as good as our latest message. Or series. Or program. And you get tired of the performing that is driven from the consuming, and sometimes you want to say, "Attractional schmactional."

We read in blogs and magazine articles that churches aren't supposed to try to keep up with or copy culture. No, we are supposed to create culture; we are actually supposed to offer things in our attractional model that haven't ever been done or seen or thought of anywhere else, because if it has, we are copying, and God forbid we do that. So we try to create, but it wears us out because sometimes we just aren't that creative. But Sunday is coming so we better think of something; and all the trying and thinking and dreaming and sometimes failing makes us want to say, "Attractional schmactional."

I've been a card-carrying, stock-buying proponent of the seeker model since the early 90s. But sometimes I get tired of catering toward seekers. Sometimes I wonder if they will ever be pleased. We do everything we can to attract their attention, speak in their language, meet their felt needs—and many of them suck from the mother church without lifting a hand to help or giving a penny to the cause. And it sometimes makes me want to say, "Attractional schmactional."

So as I was reading Alan's book on the way to Austin, I asked myself, is it "missional schmissional" or "attractional schmactional"?

Is it:

> *Do everything you can to build relationships with a friend and start spiritual conversations, hoping to lead toward a chance when you can invite them to a service where they will hear how much they matter to God?*

Or is it:

> *Be the love of Jesus right where people live, in a culture you know best where God has given you influence, and be the church? Have no expectation they will ever attend a "church in the box" service with you, but do and be the church with them, right there, where they live?*

Which is it? Which is correct? Does it have to be either/or? I whispered a prayer, "God, open my eyes."

CHAPTER 18

DEFINITIONS

This is probably a good place to stop and provide some definition for these terms. It would be worthless to write a book using these two labels over and over without clearly defining them. The rest of this book may not make sense unless you understand the terms I use and what I mean when I use them.

Missional = Sent

As a missionary, the church is sent. It does not expect non-followers to adjust their lives or cross multiple cultural boundaries to come to the church. Rather, like God sent His Son Jesus into our culture, every believer is sent to carry the mission of God into every sphere of life.

Attractional = Come to the Box

A compelling ministry built on a "come and see" model. This church does every thing it can to remove barriers and offer relevant, life-changing truth and an opportunity to enter a life of following Jesus for everyone who will come to the gathering where it is offered.

AND = Missional and Attractional

A few churches are not satisfied with the polarized debate. They don't believe a church has to be either one or the other. They believe churches can be both Missional AND Attractional. And they are pressing through the ambiguity to be both.

As the story continues, you will find God beginning to shift my understanding and my heart. The years of *Funk* likely prepared our hearts to be open to this new learning. God had let us walk through a desert so we'd be ready to learn from an Aussie about the future of the American church.

CHAPTER 19

The next two days, Rob and I sat in a hotel conference room in Austin, Texas, and listened to Alan teach for hours through the main thesis of *The Forgotten Ways* step-by-step. We had opportunity to ask questions, push back and consider the practical application for our churches.

I found myself thinking, "Yes. Yes. Yes!" over and over as I read and as Alan taught us. He was putting words to the very conversations we'd been having as a staff. He was describing exactly what we were sensing as a senior leadership team.

But it was radical. He was basically predicting the end of the effectiveness of the attractional megachurch. Not everywhere, and not over night. But he was suggesting that as America becomes more divided into smaller and smaller subcultures, the attractional model of church will become less effective.

It was exactly what I had written about two years earlier in *Pop Goes the Church*. The essence of my book was about making your attractional services more missional. I risk ridicule by quoting myself, but in the book I wrote, "It's not that people aren't pursuing their faith. There is a growing percentage of people of faith in our communities who love God the best they know how—they just see the church as completely irrelevant. It does not even cross their minds to go to a church service to figure out the next spiritual step they should take."*

There was a survey that came out around the same time my book was published that backed this up. It was conducted by Lifeway Research, and the results were published in *USA Today*. The survey found that "… a growing number of Americans are recognizing a need to develop their inner life … but many don't know where to begin, especially if they don't consider themselves 'religious.' Even if they are religious, many haven't found everything they're seeking in weekly services." The article went on to report that 86 percent said they could have a "good relationship with God without belonging to a church."†

I used that quote scores of times in talks I gave around the country in 2008 and early 2009. But, I don't think the impact of that trend hit me hard until I was sitting with Rob listening to Alan Hirsch in Austin. That is when a fundamental shift happened in my thinking. It was the first time I really considered the impact of the shrinking 40 percent.

Let me explain.

---

* Tim Stevens, *Pop Goes the Church*, (Indianapolis, IN: Power Publishing, 2008), 30.
† USAToday.com, *More Americans' Spiritual Growth Nurtured Within*, January 14, 2008, http://www.usatoday.com/news/religion/2008-01-13-spiritual-growth_N.htm

CHAPTER 20

THE SHRINKING 40%

The American church is in decline in every poll I've seen. Yes, the number of large churches is increasing, but overall church attendance continues to go down. The way we do church is working with fewer people all the time. What does "the way we do church" mean? It means the model of Christendom that has been followed for the past 1700 years. Just about every person reading this is the product of the type of church that is, as a whole, becoming less and less effective.

I'm not talking styles of worship, high church or low church, contemporary or traditional, mainline or independent or protestant or catholic. I'm talking about all of those churches combined. Just about every church in America can be described by three words: "Come to us." That is it. We put on amazing services and do everything we can to communicate truth to the people who make the effort to come to "the box" for worship. Some boxes are beautiful, and others are utilitarian. Some boxes are ornate with stained glass and a pipe organ, and others are located in an empty Walmart. But most of what we do is at, through and around "the box." Many times even the mercy and justice ministries we engage in outside the walls are done for the primary purpose of inviting people to "come to the box."

Alan Hirsch believes that this model of church still works for around 40 percent of our population. Does that mean 40 percent attend? Not at all. But there are probably around 40 percent of the population for whom the "come to us" model still works. We can put on great weekend services, and 40 percent of the people in our community are still attracted to, or at least not repelled by, that model.

Is that a scientific number? No. Is there any research to back up that number? No. But I believe it to my core.

We have asked scores of people in our church whether they think it is accurate. To make it easy to consider, we put it this way: "If you were to invite 10 people to come to church with you, how many of them do you think would consider your invitation?" Over and over, they agree that it is probably no more than four people.

Maybe the number is much lower in the northeast or northwest. Maybe it's much higher in the Bible belt states. But every pastor I have talked to agrees that the number, whatever it is, is shrinking. Whatever you decide the number is for your community, it is likely getting smaller every year.

CHAPTER 21

THE GROWING 60%

Everyone who is not in the shrinking 40 percent is part of the growing 60 percent. These are people who might believe in God (whatever that means for them), have a respect for Jesus and are on a spiritual journey, but they don't consider the church (as we know it) as a resource to help them take steps. And it is likely they never will. They pursue their spirituality through culture, friendships, music, TV personalities, their own study of the Bible, self-help books and more. A study by the Pew Forum on Religion & Public Life conducted in early 2010 said, "… more than a quarter of Americans born after 1981 have no religious preference or affiliation. Fewer than 1 in 5 teens and 20-somethings frequent worship services. But the study also reveals that young adults pray as often as their elders did at that age and share an equally strong faith in God."* More and more young adults are pursuing their faith outside of the church.

We can argue on the percentage. You may not believe it is as high as 60 percent. But whatever the number, it is growing.

And this has profound implications for the way we do church.

---

* ChicagoTribune.com, *Millenials Eschew Political, Religious Affiliation*, February 27, 2010, http://articles.chicagotribune.com/2010-02-27/news/ct-talk-pew-millennials-demo-crats-0228-20100227_1_millennials-democratic-party-young-adults

CHAPTER 22

THE HARSH TRUTH

Granger Community Church* just celebrated our 25th year. We've been a mission outpost in our community for a quarter of a century. We've seen thousands of people come to Jesus, get baptized and begin new, changed lives. The impact has been undeniable.

And yet, in February 2010, we looked at each other and asked a hard question: Is the sheer number of "unchurched" people in our area any less than it was 25 years ago before Granger existed?

Our honest answer? No. Many years ago, there was a report for our county that indicated 50% do not attend church. A report we saw recently indicated the number is now 60%. We haven't even kept up with the population growth or net loss from the decline

---

* Learn more about Granger Community Church at GCCwired.com

of other churches.

Yes, we are having an impact on individuals, and thousands have been changed. But we aren't making a dent in actually changing a growing percentage of our community into mission-minded followers of Jesus.

Once we truly accepted the truth about our impact, it seemed we had a choice to make.

1. We could continue to pour our lives and efforts and largest share of our ministry focus and dollars into reaching the 40%. Nothing wrong with that. Pure statistics show there are 62,000 people within five miles of one of our campuses who don't go to church and who are part of the 40%. That's a bunch of people who very well might be open to exploring their spirituality with us in a service.

That is certainly an option. We could probably do "successful" ministry for years with this group. But eventually, the statistical reality would catch up. And we'd be spending more money and time with decreasing effectiveness.

2. Another viable option: Leave the institutional church. Forget the attractional. It's reaching a smaller and smaller percentage every year, right? It's a dying breed. So why spend any more time there? Let's be Missional. Let's go to the masses. If the 60/40 hypothesis is true, then let's go to the more than 93,000 within

five miles of our physical sites who don't go to church and who likely will never go to church as we know it. These are people who are taking spiritual steps but need help. They are people who need to know how much they matter to God and how much they matter to the church.

It seemed like these were our choices. It has to be one or the other, right? I'd never heard of a church doing both effectively. I've heard of great churches reaching the 40 percent and a few small but effective ministries reaching the 60 percent—but I'd never heard of any church doing both.

CHAPTER 23

COMMITTED TO THE *AND*

As I wrestled with this new reality while listening to Alan Hirsch, and as I continued to study in the coming days, I became more and more convinced that God was calling Granger to the *AND*. Rob agreed. In fact, I think he was just waiting for me to catch up. We believed it didn't have to be an either/or. The fact that a church was attractional or missional was a false dichotomy.

I discovered later that the *Future Travelers* group (to which we were now firmly committed) was made up of other churches that were also trying to figure out how to live in the *AND*. They didn't know much more than we did, but they were asking the same questions. The group, including churches from Georgia, Texas, Ohio, Illinois, Washington and South Carolina, was soon to become an invaluable resource to us along the journey.

Rob and I came home from Austin totally excited and simultaneously *scared out of our wits.* Our excitement was obvious. We had found a new way to talk about the vision God had put in our hearts. We had some resources and training materials to help us lead the rest of the staff. And we knew some leaders who were asking the same questions.

Our fear? God had done a work in our hearts, and we weren't sure Mark Beeson* was going to buy in. He has said a thousand times, "Education is alienation." And we had been educated. But we were fearful it was going to alienate us from Mark. There was no way the church could move forward without the three of us marching to the same beat. It was too big of a shift. We all three had to be 100% convinced of the steps we needed to take. Anything short of that would be disastrous.

Rob and I convinced Mark to meet with the other senior leaders from *Future Travelers* to listen to Alan Hirsch in New York City in March 2010. Mark went into this meeting with the same attitude I had before Austin. He didn't want to go and agreed to only because he trusted Rob and I and we believed it was important.

In fact, we even decided to go with him. We weren't participating in the meetings, but we traveled with him to hang out with him during every break and every meal. We knew it was absolutely vital that we had time to debrief what he was learning. Rob and I made that trip to New York City with Mark, and while he was meeting, we were praying our guts out. We didn't have any idea what it would mean if Mark dismissed what he was about to learn

---

* I've talked a lot about Mark Beeson. You should follow him at MarkBeeson.com.

or determined it wasn't the right direction for Granger.

But we knew the church wasn't going to move forward without his buy-in.

CHAPTER 24

MOUNT SINAI

Two weeks before this trip to New York City, Mark had taken 12 men on a trip to Egypt. They followed the path of Moses and studied the Scripture together at key stops along the journey. For months prior to the trip, Mark had been praying and asking God to speak to him on Mount Sinai. He knew Granger was at a pivotal time, and it was a formative season for our new vision. He wanted desperately to hear from God about our next steps as a church or his next steps as a leader. We were all praying with him.

His experience was totally different than he anticipated. It was a long journey up the mountain, and quite to his surprise, he physically had a difficult time making it to the top. Mark is in great health, but a combination of the terrain and extreme temperatures forced him to stop for a break several times. At one point, he thought he might not make it and would have to stay and wait for the other guys to come back down. But the men supported each other, and everyone in the group was finally able to make it to the top for a time of prayer and reading Scripture.

But Mark didn't hear from God on Mount Sinai. At least he didn't think so at first, and he was disappointed. It had been his prayer for months. His heart was ready. His ears were open. It didn't make sense to him why God didn't speak.

As the trip progressed, Mark began to realize that God actually did speak to him. He shared his learning with me a few days after returning: "God showed me how much I need the team around me. I can't make it to the top of the next mountain on my own." That was very interesting to me, because Mark has been a team player as long as I've known him. He didn't build the church around his personality—he built it around the mission. He has never gone anywhere alone. He's always been a huge proponent of finding great people and handing off ministry. So for the big learning to be, "You need others," well, it didn't seem that earth-shattering to me. But as I reflected on it later, and especially while in New York City, I think a shift was happening inside of Mark.

In the past, Mark would lead us toward a challenge and have an amazing team all around him. And when I say "amazing team," I'm talking about uber-talented, high capacity, world-changing leaders. But clearly, he was in front leading the way. I think God may have been telling Mark on Mount Sinai, "For this next challenge, you will no longer be leading the charge from the front. Instead you will have the rest of your team at your side, arm-in-arm, leading with you. And right on the front lines beside you will be hundreds of men and women in the church who will also be leading."

I believe it was this Mount Sinai experience that prepared him for New York City and Alan Hirsch. As we got back on the plane at Newark to fly home, I think Mark was probably only 75 percent convinced of what he had heard and experienced. He was thinking about church in different ways and had his mind stretched. But he wasn't drinking the Kool-Aid yet. Not completely.

But that didn't matter. He was 110 percent convinced that Rob and I were partners with him in the ministry. And because of his experience on Mount Sinai, he was tuned in to listening to where God was leading us more than perhaps ever before. And so together we made the decision to move forward.

CHAPTER 25

TRAINING THE LEADERS

We returned from New York City and decided to begin taking the other pastors and staff through some of the learning that we had experienced. That was a huge step for us. Up until this point, it was a journey contained to our senior team. Now we were opening it up for our top-tier leaders.

We bought them all copies of *The Forgotten Ways* and set up a training time to work through the book together. We read chapters, watched online videos of Alan teaching the content and discussed what we were learning.

Just before we started the first session, Mark said to me, "I think we are opening a can." I said, "Yep, and once it's opened, we will never be able to close it." We talked for a few minutes about whether we should open it. We didn't know exactly what it meant yet, but we knew this journey was irreversible. We knew that once we began to make room for these conversations among our leaders, we would never be able to go back to "church" as we knew it.

It shouldn't have surprised us, but for most of our leaders, *The Forgotten Ways* material was not new information. God had been doing something in the hearts of our leaders for years. It had been building to this point. This content, however, gave us new terminology and a common way to talk about it.

We also made the decision to cancel the *Innovate Conference* scheduled for the fall of 2010. It was an annual conference we had been doing since 2002 that drew hundreds of church leaders who wanted inspiration and practical help. We decided to put it on the shelf*, and instead we began designing a conference we were going to call **AND**. It wasn't so much because we sensed an overwhelming desire from our constituents for the conference. It's because WE needed the conference, and it was a way to pull others into our conversation about how to be churches that are intentionally attractional AND missional. More than 200 of our own leaders from Granger attended the conference, along with 400 church leaders from around the country.

Every day through 2010 brought new realizations and a firmer resolve. At one point while Mark was sitting in my office, he said, "Everything I've thought about church for 40 years is changing. And I'm not sure I like it." That sums up what all of us were feeling. It was unsettling to be questioning the very core of how the church communicates the Gospel. It was scary to think that the method and model to which all of us had committed years of our lives was becoming less and less effective. And it was intimidating to realize we had to move forward into an area where no maps had yet been drawn.

---

* Beginning in September 2012, we launched the conference again. Check it out at ReInnovateConference.com

But we had no choice. God was clearly calling us into new territory. We weren't going alone, though. We would soon find out that the congregation was also sensing a new trajectory for Granger Community Church.

CHAPTER 26

SHAPING THE VISION

During the 12 months following January 2010, we worked hard on a process* that involved every person in the church. I think the only way to describe this season would be to compare it to the birth of a baby.

Every day during the "pregnancy" we were working hard to make preparations. We were gathering feedback from thousands of people; then going back to them again to get more feedback; then drafting the vision and going back to ask they what they thought; then revising the vision and going back with another version; then finalizing and giving them an opportunity to ask questions. About nine months into the process, we had the same feeling that probably every mom in the world does when she's at the end of her

---

* You will find this process described in detail beginning in Part Two on page 159.

term—we just wanted to get the baby out! Except we weren't done. The process still had three more months before it would be complete.

During this season, we started feeling *The Big Mo* again. Although the process was long and thorough, every step helped to fan the flame that was beginning to rage. As our marching orders became clearer with each step and each revision, we were getting the real sense that people were saying, "Let's just get started!"

I had a real fear that what happened next had the potential to derail all of our progress.

CHAPTER 27

A THREE-MONTH SABBATICAL

For years we had been trying to bless Mark Beeson with a sabbatical. He had been doing full-time, non-stop ministry for nearly 40 years without an extended break. We finally were able to secure a grant (thanks to the Lilly Endowment*) that would fund his sabbatical, and I think that gave us the leverage we needed to convince him that it would be a good time. So by the middle of 2009, we had scheduled his sabbatical for fall 2010.

Little did we know his sabbatical would fall right in the middle of writing a new five-year vision.

So when he left at the beginning of September 2010, and we knew he wouldn't be returning for three months, I was concerned.

---

* See LillyEndowment.org for more information.

My fear had nothing to do with the ability of the team to continue the process in his absence. I also wasn't concerned that the church would be just as healthy upon his return as when he left. Mark had not allowed the church to be built around his abilities alone. The rest of the pastors and staff would lead well.

My great trepidation was because of how well I knew Mark. He is a dreamer and a visionary. He never stops thinking up new ways to make an impact. He is a verbal processor, constantly talking to anyone who will listen to his newest idea or strategy or dream. He relies heavily on the team around him to filter his ideas.

Here was my fear, plain and simple: *Mark was going to continue to dream and plan for three months without anyone on the team to bounce his ideas off. In the meantime, the senior team was going to continue to take steps and make strides toward developing a new vision over the next three months. It was quite possible our senior team would be in an ENTIRELY different place than Mark at the end of three months. And that would be disastrous.*

But there was nothing I could do control the outcome. Above all, I was committed to doing everything I could to let Mark reconnect with God and his family so that he would come back with great health and energy for the next ministry season. I instructed our staff to let Mark relax: "If you see Mark over the next three months, tell him everything is great. Lie if you have to!"

During the first two months, I didn't see Mark at all and only talked to him twice, very briefly. But at the beginning of his third month away, Mark showed up unexpectedly at our weekly senior team meeting. As he walked toward our table (in a restaurant where we were meeting), I took our meeting agenda and slid it under the table. I then texted everyone else sitting around the table and said, "Remember, everything is great! No talk about work stuff!" I didn't want Mark to get pulled back into the details. He still had a month remaining.

As his sabbatical came to a conclusion, I had been praying and asking God to somehow keep his heart and dreams, and our progress on the vision, in perfect sync with each other. I knew it would be a miracle. I also knew the trauma of reentry could be significant. We had been running the church completely without his leadership for 90 days. I wanted the smoothest transition possible for him to return to his role as our senior leader.

During his first week back, I did three things that I was hoping would minimize the difficult transition. First, I set up an online document that everyone on the senior team began contributing to that contained a summary of key decisions or events that happened in his absence. This ended up being 17 pages long but proved invaluable in bringing him up-to-speed on everything he needed to know. And it likely saved him multiple weeks with hours of meetings.

Secondly, I scheduled a three-hour meeting, just him and me, on his first day back. This was a chance to hear stories, share hearts and give him an overview of the progress we'd made on the vision while he was gone. I also had a chance to find out what he had been thinking and dreaming about while he was spending time with family and God.

And last, I scheduled an all-day meeting with the whole senior team. We called it the "Reentry Meeting." He showed us pictures of his trips and talked about adventures along the way. He asked questions about stuff that had transpired while he was gone. And we walked through the most recent draft of the Vision.

By the end of that all-day meeting, I realized the impossible had happened. Even though Mark had been gone for three months, our entire senior team was still in perfect harmony on our future. We remained in lock step on pursuing a vision that would radically change the trajectory of the church.

It was a flat-out miracle.

CHAPTER 28

THE VISION IS COMPLETE

It had been exactly one year since we made the decision to put our ideas about the vision on a shelf and listen to what God was saying to the people of Granger Community Church.

A businessman, whom none of us had ever met, offered us his home for the location of our January 2011 planning retreat. It would prove to be quite a different setting than the previous year. Instead of being in a small cabin 45 minutes from Granger, this retreat would find us in a multi-million dollar, oceanfront estate in a remote village in Baja, Mexico. The lodging and all the food for the week was completely paid for by this businessman. And on top of that, some families from Granger paid for the plane tickets for the senior team (and spouses!) to get there. Another miracle!

I don't want to be mystical, but it was almost as if God was giving us that setting as a symbol of His favor on the vision that was emerging. We spent two full days finalizing the vision. We labored over every single word to make sure it communicated clearly. We closed our time with our spouses on a courtyard overlooking the Sea of Cortez, praying and committing the vision to Him.

We were sure the 2016 Vision was right. We believed it to our core. But it was with great anxiety that we returned from Mexico to begin communicating this final vision to the church. We knew there was huge risk involved in saying, "We are done. Here is the vision." Up until that point, it had just been brainstorming. We hadn't committed to anything yet. It was just ideas on paper. But now, we were throwing all our credibility on the line and staking our futures on this vision.

We were all in. There was no going back.

CHAPTER 29

BE THE CHURCH

Before everything else, and at the core of this new vision, was our belief that the church is not an institution, and it is not a building. It is a movement of people who understand that they are Jesus' plan to transform and heal communities. This was the first pillar of our 2016 Vision:

The number of people being the Church in their neighborhoods, schools, cafés and communities seven days a week will outnumber the casual Christians just going to church.

Every follower of Jesus has a "missional impulse" within them; we will help believers in the GCC family discover and activate this impulse to make a difference in their world.

We will equip Christ-followers to leverage their leadership and expertise in every domain of society (justice, education, healthcare, government, religion, business and the arts).

We will transition children and student ministries into a holistic family ministry, partnering with parents to disciple their children and students for 936 weeks—from the time a child is born until they turn eighteen.

We will find, celebrate and tell stories of our people "being" the Church at every opportunity.

I remember hearing Dave Ferguson* say that "every believer has a *missional impulse*" for the first time at the AND Conference in 2010. It is such an anti-institutional idea but so resonated with me. It is our inclination as church leaders to think it is our job to set the agenda and ask people to join us. We decide to feed the homeless or offer sports clinics or teach a Bible study or take care of babies. "These are the things the church offers—you can volunteer your gifts in one of these areas," we say. And, because actions speak louder than words, what people often hear is: "If you don't like what we are doing, go find another church."

I totally understand there are certain functions that a gathered church needs to provide, and it requires skilled volunteers to jump in and help. We should keep doing those things and inviting others to join us.

But we can't stop there! Our commitment is to figure out how to help each individual find their God-given missional impulse.

---

* Dave (DaveFerguson.org) is the lead pastor of Community Christian Church in Naperville, Illinois, and founder of New Thing Network (NewThing.org).

God has gifted *everyone* to be able to influence and help someone else take a step toward Jesus. And these may be people who will never be reached through a public service at Granger Community Church. There may be thousands of different groups that become the focus of our congregation, such that we would never be able to fund or organize them all. That's okay as long as we are offering training and support.

We are going to give an extra emphasis organizationally to these seven established domains of society: justice, education, healthcare, government, religion, business and the arts. What if we gathered every follower of Jesus from Granger who works in the field of health and medicine and asked them to begin dreaming how, as a group and as individuals, they could bring positive change to our community? We don't tell them what *we* are going to do. No, instead we provide the space and let *them* bring the solutions. And what if we gathered every school teacher, principal and college educators together and asked them to begin dreaming together how they might be able to transform our school systems with the love of Jesus and the power of their combined knowledge and influence? Can you imagine the change that could come with a laser-focused effort from people in each of these seven areas?

Specifically in the arena of the family, we began to re-think our approach to children and student ministries. Our focus has mostly been on the hour or two that the child is in the building each week, and we believe we've knocked the ball out of the park in that hour.

But, we began to envision a future where we are doing as much to help parents lead their children spiritually at home as we are investing in teaching while the kids are with us. This will impact our staff and our priorities as we press into the future.

At the foundation of all of this, we realized we needed to do a hundred times better at telling stories. Concepts are hard to understand, but stories bring them to life. We can preach this new vision until we are blue in the face, but until we start telling stories, we will have difficulty making it the new normal. We decided that during the next five years, and especially in the first few, we would tell an imbalanced proportion of stories that illustrated our preferred future. As those stories are elevated, it will awaken the imagination in our people to create their own.

CHAPTER 30

ACTIVATE THE CAMPUS

Most outsiders would describe our buildings and property as very attractional. That is, they have been designed mostly around the weekend service. A vast proportion of the capital budget over the years has been spent to provide a great experience for 2,000 people at a time to experience a 70-minute service, along with great classrooms for their children to learn and of course adequate parking (since most of them refuse to walk). And although we do offer some events, classes and activities during the week, they tend to happen within the restraints of what we've built for the weekend experience.

In essence, the campus serves the 40 percent. It is perfectly designed to reach the people in our community who are most like us. And for years, it has been very effective at doing so.

But, we were learning, it is not designed well to do much else. We decided that needed to change in our 5-year vision and wrote this as the second pillar:

We will have remodeled the Granger campus and programs to help not just our congregation, but the greater community, with Jesus at the center.

The Granger campus will become a gathering place for the community. We will build a chapel to help people through life-defining moments with inspirational architecture. We will build a Commons where people meet and friends gather. We will add paths, benches, pavilions, fireplaces and water features that invite people to enjoy the beauty of God's creation.

We will utilize our fabulous Children's Center and launch a weekday faith-based preschool and/or daycare to meet the growing needs of parents as they try to raise their kids with virtue.

Like Monroe Circle Community Center has done for a neighborhood in South Bend and like this remodel will do for Michiana, every location or gathering in our growing GCC network will exist for the unique transformation and elevation of the neighborhood, village, city or region where they are located.

There is a common belief in the movement toward Missional Communities that church buildings are bad. I don't believe that for a second. I believe church buildings can be a huge blessing, and they can also be a huge burden.

I think one of the primary problems with churches that own

buildings is that people begin to think that the church *is* a building. We say, "Invite your friend to church" or "Be sure you come to church this weekend," as though the building is the church. But we don't really mean that. We mean to say, "You are the church. The church isn't a building. The church is the people of God." So which is it? Am I the church, or is this building the church?

We call the property the "church campus" but then say it's a place to offer help to the community. Wouldn't that be like calling my home the "Stevens' House" and then trying to convince people it is open to everyone? Sure doesn't sound very open.

So deep within this vision to activate the campus is a plan to turn all the terminology upside down. What if the "church campus" was called *Harbor Ridge*? (This isn't a real name, just a placeholder for sake of illustration). But imagine if the entire community knew that *Harbor Ridge* was the place you go for hope and healing. People want groceries, they think of Kroger or Jewel. People want clothes and they think of Target or the mall. People need medical attention, they might think of the 24-Hour Medical Center. What if, in the same way, people thought of *Harbor Ridge* as the place in the community they go for hope and healing, at their moments of greatest need.

Need help with your marriage? There are classes and counseling available at *Harbor Ridge* led by followers of Jesus. Need help figuring out how to be a great parent? There is coaching available at *Harbor Ridge* that is based on Scripture. You ask, "Why not just say those things are at the church?" Because most people in our society don't see the church as a viable place to go for help. Many people, especially those in the 60 percent, would never consider visiting a church. If it's at the church—they won't go. But if it's at Harbor Ridge—is it possible they might visit?

Need help with your kids because you both work? Bring them to the daycare or preschool at *Harbor Ridge*. Are your finances a mess? Catch a Financial Peace University class at *Harbor Ridge*. Struggling with addictions? Recovering from the loss of a child? The first thought that would come to your mind, "I bet *Harbor Ridge* has something that could help me."

The place you think of at the biggest moments of transition or crisis in your life—such as weddings or funerals – you think of *The Chapel at Harbor Ridge*.

And every function, every event, every interaction with every guest is filled with faith and love and spiritual intentionality. People who come to Harbor Ridge for anything walk away having been touched by the love and grace of a Jesus-follower.

Oh, and where does Granger Community Church meet? Lots of places all over our community, but in *Granger,* we meet at *Harbor Ridge*.

We think this change in terminology will help the community. But we also believe it will help to reinforce to our people that *they* are the church. And they cannot be contained in a building.

This is not just theory. We are taking concrete steps to do the following over the next five years:

- Build a chapel that can serve the community for weddings and funerals and be a place they can pray or find solace in times of need.
- Open a café that is open to the community for meals or drinks seven days a week.
- Provide running paths, trails, benches and water features throughout the property to give

a way for people to enjoy God's creation in an
area that is largely paved.

- Open a licensed, high-quality, faith-based, early
  childhood learning center that will become a
  teaching model for other centers around
  the country.
- Turn a portion of our property over to a devel-
  oper to establish an Artisan's Village of retail
  pads for dance, music or art studios, architec-
  tural or graphic design companies and other
  arts-related small businesses, bringing more
  people from the community onto the campus.
- Open a 7-day-a-week retail location offering books, music and inspirational home
  décor, providing a much-needed outlet in our
  community.
- Offer facility space for community events, such
  as an area college graduation that has moved
  to our campus or the public high school dance
  that recently took place in our auditorium.
- Give the campus a new name and brand that
  will encompass this new community-centric
  focus.

Just like we've seen happen at the Monroe Circle Community
Center in South Bend, we believe it's possible to turn our church
buildings into centers for community transformation.

CHAPTER 31

REPRODUCE AT EVERY LEVEL

This final pillar of our 2016 Vision can be boiled down to discipleship. That is an oft-misunderstood term. But we have come to believe that spiritual maturity is not about what you know. It's not even about what you do. Spiritual maturity = reproduction.

Every follower of Jesus will be a reproducing follower of Jesus. And every church will be a reproducing church.

We will offer life-changing gatherings for worship and teaching in our current locations and launch three additional sites in our region with 9,000 gathering as one church in five locations.

We will raise the temperature for life-on-life discipleship so it is normal for people to become reproducing followers of Jesus by owning their personal growth. Consumer-oriented Christians will, by design, not feel comfortable long-term.

We will distribute high-quality content wherever and whenever it is needed. At any time we will be able to teach, train and inspire thousands of people as they gather from their home, church, business, or wherever they are located.

We will launch and equip Granger Community Church start-ups all over the globe. All expressions—micro, mega, multi, rural, suburban, urban, multi-ethnic, local, domestic and international—will be united by the same mission and DNA. We will be a movement of more than 100,000 missional followers of Jesus gathering as 2,000 reproducing churches.

Did you read that line? *Consumer-oriented Christians will, by design, not feel comfortable long-term.* How many Christians are consumer-oriented? All of us. There are times that I'm consumer-oriented, and there are times when you are also. Admit it. We all need help to move out of our comfort zones and be pushed toward growth.

The last paragraph is all about starting churches. We call them "start-ups" because we know the average person doesn't see himself or herself as a church planter. If we say, "How many people want to start a church?" we will see very few hands. Why? Because they think they have to be like Bill Hybels or Mark Beeson to start a church.

But we are determined to change the definition of a church. That's why we list all expressions of a church—micro, mega, multi-site, rural, suburban, urban, multi-ethnic, local, domestic and international. In *The Forgotten Ways*, Alan Hirsch says there are five things that define a church:

- **A covenanted community** – *a church is formed not by people just hanging out together but ones bound together in a distinctive bond. There is a certain obligation toward one another formed around covenant.*
- **Centered on Jesus** – *He is the new covenant with God and he thus forms as the true epicenter of an authentic Christian faith … a covenant community centered around Jesus participates in the salvation that he brings. We receive the grace of God in Him.*

But, Hirsch continues, more is required to truly constitute a church. *A true encounter with God in Jesus must result in:*

- **Worship,** *defined as offering our lives back to God through Jesus.*
- **Discipleship,** *defined as following Jesus and becoming increasingly like him (Christlikeness)*
- **Mission**, *defined as extending the mission of God through the activities of his people.* *

That's it. A church doesn't require buildings or Sunday morning services. You don't need a website or paid staff members. We've seen this work successfully in more than a thousand start-up

---

* Alan Hirsch, *The Forgotten Ways,* (Grand Rapids, MI: Brazos Press, 2006), 40-41.

churches in southern India. We are committed to figuring out how to do it also in our American neighborhoods.

Mark Beeson coined the term "Essential Churches" during this process. It really gets at what we mean. We are going to boil everything down to the essential of what church is and then equip believers to start hundreds and even thousands of them.

Why? Because everyone can't (or won't) come to Granger, Indiana. We are going to have a limited impact on our world if we just continue to do church as we've always done at 630 East University Drive. Reproduction is a non-negotiable, and it may be the word driving us more than anything.

And honestly, it scares the bejeebers out of us. EVERY follower is reproducing. EVERY church is reproducing. Talk about a daunting task.

There is no way this is possible if we keep doing church the way we've always done it. And once you start changing stuff, people are going to misunderstand. Some might even leave the church.

ROB WEGNER: PASTOR OF LIFE MISSION

During the same season we felt stuck in our "Jerusalem," our expression in Judea, Samaria and the ends of the Earth was exploding. While "church as institution" was struggling at home, "church as movement" was off the charts.

Starting in 2001, our church found a new home in India. From the first meeting of 15 people in a run-down YWCA, over time, deep friendships were formed. For the first five years, we worked alongside church planters trained by the Bible League to provide advanced training to help those churches move out of the start-up phase into health and repro-duction. By 2006, we began to oversee the church planting directly. Our shared dream was to plant a church in an otherwise unreached village and then equip and empower that church to become the hub for com-munity development. We knew that if the Kingdom of God came to a community, it would elevate every domain of society: health, education, housing, employment, justice, arts, family life and more.

A few years into our church planting initiative, the movement went into multiplication mode. The new normal was reproduction. Within 24 months, the average church was a reproducing church. In one six-month window alone, more than 250 churches were planted in homes, under banyan trees and in public spaces. Make no mistake. These simple churches were not small groups. They were led by ordinary revolutionar-ies and were fully functional churches that worship, serve, meet, study, do life and lead others to Jesus—together.

Through church-planting in India and our community center in Monroe Circle*, we began to learn about church as movement. Our missional imagination was on fire. We began to dream about what could happen if we could find a way to let that convergence define us *wherever we are*. We began to see it—the church as apostolic movement.

Now that we had tasted the fruit of what was possible, we had to ask ourselves how it might be possible to plant the seeds of that kind of revolution in Granger.

That's what led to the wildly collaborative process of visioneering that Tim is describing. It might seem ambitious to dream that "every follower of Jesus will be a reproducing follower of Jesus, and every church will be a reproducing church." But we have seen it happen!

Up to this point, the changes we have made as a church happened with-in the attractional ("come to the box") paradigm. The process of shifting to another paradigm—church as movement—has been something of a phenomenon for us all."

---

*   See chapter 11 for the story of the Monroe Circle Community Center.

CHAPTER 32

CRITICS

Even as the momentum was building toward the new vision, there were plenty of critics who were making their dislike heard. Some were upset because we were messing with their comfort. Others felt like we weren't going far enough in our efforts to be missional.

We heard from a few who believed we were putting too much money into expanding the campus, not understanding that it was in an effort to reorient the campus toward the community. There were others who loved that we were putting money into the Chapel and Commons but had no idea what "missional communities" were and why they required money to launch.

Mark received an especially difficult email from a leader who believed we weren't "willing to sacrifice some of our desires and comforts to reach our friends where they live." This was hurtful since it was the exact opposite of what we were trying to do, and this leader had refused to participate in some meetings where the vision would be explained—where he'd have a chance to ask questions.

Another guy couldn't believe we were raising money for a chapel. He wrote, "To use that money in the community would be so much more helpful, … I feel like we are going in the wrong direction and I can no longer support it." For him, we hadn't been effective in communicating that we were changing our campus to be a center *for* the community.

I remember a very difficult few days when I had to dismiss a friend from staff who I had worked with for more than a decade. She had done nothing wrong, but we didn't believe she had the leadership capacity to take her ministry to where it needed to go with the new vision. She left quietly, but there were some hateful words and critical accusations made in the few days following that decision by others who didn't understand. I remember walking into our staff meeting that week wondering if there was anyone around who still liked me. It's a juvenile thing to admit, but I'd taken so many hits the day before, that is honestly what I was feeling.

I share these stories not so you will feel sorry for us but to illustrate that you will always run into critics when you do something big for God. It doesn't matter what it is—there will always be people who would rather stay where they are. There will always be a few who will think you are the Devil for trying to do something new and different. Many times they will spiritualize it, and others will hear that you are doing something unbiblical. Sometimes they just don't agree, but rather than quietly refrain from participating they loudly voice their disapproval.

I think too often churches get side-tracked by the "no" votes. We cater to their whining and spend all our energy trying to keep them happy. Or we spend all our time in damage control because of the side conversations they are having. Don't get me wrong; I think it's important to listen. Sometimes (perhaps often) God will speak through someone when we least expect it. But there is a cross-over point after we've listened, considered and prayed. We know what God has called the church to do and be—and we must pursue that with confidence.

Some will go with us. And some won't. And we'll experience deep pain, sometimes, when the person who chooses to leave is our closest friend or relative, the person who we never imagined moving on without.

My advice? Just put one foot in front of the other. Count "yes" votes, and keep moving.

And someday, God might just bless you with the shock of your life.

CHAPTER 33

AN UNEXPECTED MEETING

The church has been around since 1986. We have taken offerings every week, we have always had a special Christmas offering and we have occasionally raised money for a project through a stewardship campaign. We have a lot of history of raising money to invest in ministry.

Several times we have worked with professional consultants, and they always look at our church, review our numbers and then tell us that if we are going to reach our goal, we will need to have a significant pledge from several families in the church. In fact, they very specifically tell us something like this: "You will need to have one family give $1 million, and you'll need to have three or four families give in the range of $300k to $500k." And we just look at the consultants and nod and smile, because never in our history have we received a gift of that size. We remind them that we are not located in southern California or Miami or Houston or the suburbs of Chicago. *"We live in South Flippin' Bend. People don't stay here if they want to make a bunch of money,"* we remind them.

And yet every time, we pray our guts out for a gift of that size. But year after year, the ministry continues to grow because a whole bunch of "average" people do what they can. That is how the church has been built. And we have been so grateful that we have a broad, grass-roots buy-in from hundreds of families in the region.

Like every year, we were praying again for a sizable gift. We believed the vision was big enough for someone to invest in a huge way. I didn't know Mark was going to do this, but in early March 2011, Mark publicly told the church he was specifically praying for a family to give $1 million toward the 2016 vision. Even though we've prayed for a gift of that size for years, up until that service, Mark had never felt the release to say it out loud to the weekend crowd. I'm not often caught off guard by things he says, since we process nearly everything together. But this was a surprise. I thought it was very interesting that he decided to tell the congregation that we were praying for a sizable gift.

It was two days after Mark had told the church he was praying for a $1 million gift. I had just returned from a lunch meeting and had messages waiting for me from a couple whom I had never met. They were five minutes away and asked if they could come right over to ask some questions about the vision and *The New Normal Project* (this was the project we launched to raise money for the 2016 Vision).

We had an amazing conversation, talking about life, faith, their story and the new vision that Granger is chasing. They brought with them a copy of our brochure where we outlined the new 2016 Vision. Looking at it in this man's hands was like seeing a well-worn book. They had taken it home from the weekend series when we shared the 2016 Vision for the first time and had been living in it, reading every word over and over. They were astounded at how closely their own spiritual journey aligned with the vision that we were presenting to the congregation.

The man leaned forward and asked me with intensity, "Have you ever known that God was speaking directly to you?" He went on to tell me that this had happened to him three or four times in his life. He told me the story of a few of these times when God had given him and his wife significant direction. Each time, he explained, his hands would sweat.

The next thing this man did was ask me to leave the room.

You have to remember, we were sitting in *my* office. He was asking me to leave my office! Kind of funny, but he wanted to talk to his wife in private.

I stood outside my office for a few minutes, still having no idea why we were having this conversation. All I knew was this was a couple that was totally captured by the vision God had given the church. This was exactly what we'd been praying for as we spent months working on every word. Although I'd never met them, they seemed like the type of couple who might eventually lead a missional community.

They call me back into my office, and he continued his story: "This past weekend, when Mark said he was praying for a family to give $1 million, my hands got all sweaty, and I knew exactly what God wanted us to do." At this point, I was thinking something spiritual, like "no-flippin-way!"

He continued, "We believe God wants us to commit $1 million to the church for this new vision."

I have no idea what I said next. I think I may have actually said "No-flippin-way!", I'm not sure. I'm not an emotional person, but at that moment I felt as close to tears as I ever have with total strangers. I had goosebumps on every inch of my body and was somewhat in shock.

After we finished the meeting, I sat in my office for a few minutes soaking in what had just happened. I immediately wrote down the following disconnected thoughts while I was still absorbing what had just happened:

"We have talked for more than a year how there will be people who will be drawn to the church because of the vision. These people have been completely captured by the vision of where God is taking us. How affirming!"

"What would have happened if I had not responded to their message, or had been too busy to meet with them, or had encouraged them to drop me an email rather than stopping by the office?"

"Why now? Why did God wait 25 years to give us a million-dollar commitment? What does this mean?"

"Sometimes, in my flesh, I think, 'If God is going to give us $1 million, it's going to come from one of these three people.' Like I can figure it out. And yet this came from someone who wouldn't have been on any of my lists. God is so much bigger than anything we can manage or strategize or manipulate."

"This is just the beginning. We've been putting in so much work over the past year with very little tangible response. This commit-

ment feels like God just returned our homework with a smiley face on it. And yet I think it is just the beginning of what God is going to do with and through us."

The following day, I was met in the lobby with an envelope containing a check for one million dollars from people I had never even met two days earlier. We kept it very quiet for a few days while we waited for the check to clear—but then gladly announced to the church this outrageous step of faith and generosity. It was a huge boost of momentum for the church, giving us clear confirmation that we were on the right path.

It was just the first of many blessings that would come in those early days of 2011.

CHAPTER 34

AMAZING BLESSINGS

In the weeks and months that followed that outrageous gift, we saw so many instances when God surprised us again and again. We were able to bring two people on staff as a result of the new vision who are better hires than we ever imagined possible. I'm talking world-class leaders to help us put feet to the vision.

The congregation "bought in" to *The New Normal Project* in an unprecedented way. More people invested up front to the project than in any previous campaign in the history of the church—both in dollar amount and percentage. And their giving has continued to stay very strong all the way through the printing of this book.

We received two unsolicited gifts in the general offerings that were each larger than any previous single gift.

And then in May, we received another reality-busting phone call. A local church was asking if they could give us their facility, well-maintained and free and clear of any debt. It was a gift valued at $1.2 million and located in THE perfect neighborhood for our multisite congregation in Elkhart, Indiana. We opened the doors on that facility in December 2011, and by March of 2012, we had seen the congregation grow by 67%.

MARK WALTZ: PASTOR OF CONNECTIONS

I'll never forget May 24, 2011. That's the day the phone call came in: "We have a church building in Elkhart we'd love to talk to Granger Community about." That was it. A day later my friend Don and I toured the building and property. The leaders were very clear: They were seeking to give their property to GCC-Elkhart. I was stunned. Give? Unbelievable. Four acres, a 50-year-old, well maintained building nestled in a residential community — given to us.

As a church, we thought we might need a new place to meet, but owning a building wasn't in our prayer list. We believed we'd like to be within the city limits, but my prayer wasn't that specific. We had prayed for God to extend our reach, to give us the city, but ... By August 2011, we'd witnessed the signing of the deed — a million-dollar plus asset. Generously given.

The people of St. John's United Church of Christ, a 122-year ministry in Elkhart, humbled us with their generosity and their vision. They wanted what we wanted: Jesus to be honored and people to be drawn to Him. This momentous gift came just three months after our largest single cash donation. Mark Beeson had been clear in a vision cast related to our 2016 vision. "We have never had a million-dollar donation given for any cause in the history of our church. But, I believe that million-dollar gift is here." Within one week that donor stepped forward. He'd not merely heard Mark Beeson speak with hope; he'd heard God speak directly to him and his wife.

Not one but two gifts equaling more than two million dollars within three months. Clearly, God was up to something. Money isn't the only measure of God's work, but without it, ministry can be short-circuited. We were experiencing the favor of God. He was working modern day miracles right in front of us.

Amazing.

Those early indications gave us confidence in the new vision. Just walking the halls, you could sense a different vibe from the congregation. There was a true sense that God was preparing us for the days ahead.

Of course, you can never see too far down the road. And sometimes the path is ripe with obstacles. On Thanksgiving Day 2011, it was like all hell broke loose.

CHAPTER 35

TRAGEDY AND PAIN

I cannot adequately explain the depths of the pain that began in November 2011. But I attempted to in a letter to Satan that I published on my blog* in mid-December:

Dear Satan,

It's not going to work. I'm on to you. We are on to you.

I know you are not omni-present. You can only be in one place at a time. For decades I've watched you wreak havoc around the world, but rarely have I felt you in my town, messing with my friends, focused on my church. But it seems like you planted yourself squarely at our doorstep over the

* LeadingSmart.com, *Dear Satan*, December 13, 2011, http://www.leadingsmart. com/2011/12/dear-satan.html.

past few weeks. It's almost like Someone said to you, "Consider my servants in Granger–there are many there who follow Me without question. And I am getting ready to do some really big stuff through them."

And so you came. And you might still be here.

- *Two weeks ago I learned that a friend on our staff lost his mother. She died suddenly the day after Thanksgiving.*
- *Two days later I learned that a couple on our staff is struggling through the very scary reality of breast cancer.*
- *The next day I learn that my sister's husband has been diagnosed with ALS. No cure.*
- *Then I learn that one of my closest friends–a guy who I thought I'd be working beside for the next 20 years–can no longer stay on our staff.*
- *A day later, another friend finds she may be facing skin cancer.*
- *The next day, one of our senior team members drops suddenly to the sidewalk vomiting, and spends the night in the ER.*
- *Then he learns a couple days later that his grandma died.*
- *Then this morning we learn that Mark Beeson's mom died quickly and unexpectedly.*

I realize that much of this is the natural progression

of life and death, and you can't be blamed for every bit of sickness and disease. But I believe you are trying to distract us. You are trying to get our eye off the ball. You are trying to shake us to our core.

There are moments, sometimes hours, even days, when I think it's working. I am shaken to my core. It's hard to keep putting one foot in front of the other. It's hard to see the hand of God.

Like last Tuesday night when I sat with hundreds of students and parents as they learned their youth pastor would no longer be their youth pastor–that the man they looked up to had let them down. At that moment, it was hard to see the hand of God. Instead, I saw your hand. Someone said to me, "All things work together for good!" But I wasn't ready to hear that. I watched a row of high school girls in front of me hear the news as tears streamed down their faces, and I wanted to scream. I imagined you standing in the back of the room with a grin on your face.

Two days ago I sat with my brother-in-law and sister, as he told his church that he is facing a life-ending illness–and quite possibly has a very short amount of time to live. I looked around at the teens in his church, who he has led faithfully for 12 years, as they learned for the first time of their pastor's disease. And I wondered if you were in the back of the room, praying to whoever you pray to that the faith of these kids would be irreparably shaken: "Surely they won't follow a God that allows this to happen."

At the end of that service, I sat next to my sister as the congregation was led to sing "Blessed Be The Name of the Lord." Honestly, I wasn't ready to sing it. My heart was too heavy. My strength too sapped. So if that was your goal, then put a point in your column.

But you need to know, you aren't going to win. I don't have the energy right now to pray some Heavenly words of faith against you. But I know in my heart that you are the ultimate loser. You may discourage us; you may win some battles; you may cause some to lose their way; you may distract us for a season; you may even take people away from us that we love–but in the end, you lose.

Since I know you hate Scripture, let me quote some:

> *"We are pressed on every side by troubles, but we are not crushed and broken. We are perplexed, but we don't give up and quit. We are hunted down, but God never abandons us. We get knocked down, but we get up again and keep going." (2 Corinthians 4:8-9).*

I am convinced more than ever that God is preparing to unleash His power and work through the people of Granger Community Church like never before.

I would suggest you get out of the way.

I'm sure there are some theological reasons that I shouldn't be writing Satan a letter. Don't worry, I didn't send it. But it's the best way to communicate to you the depths of the pain that we went through just as the vision was beginning to get some traction.

As a team, we took a huge blow to the gut, and it knocked us down. It is now three months later, and we still haven't fully recovered. It will likely be another three-to six-months before we'll be back on track emotionally and organizationally, with the people in place who are needed to help us see the vision become reality.

But one thing hasn't changed, and that is our resolve. We know that God has given us a clear picture of our future, and we have an enemy who is bent on our destruction. It would be disingenuous to say this recent season didn't slow us down. It did. Our progress slowed down dramatically. But we are getting back up to fight again.

Given the choice, I would have skipped the pain of the past few months without blinking. Looking back even farther, I also would have taken a pass on the *Jolt* and the season of *Funk*. I would have rather we had kept the *Big Mo* and not lost it. I wish I hadn't lost so many friends during the season when we couldn't pay them or the times people left out of frustration with our direction.

I don't ever want to go again through the deep pain of relational stress when I had no idea if I was winning or trusted or wanted—and when my closest friend didn't know the same from me. I don't want to repeat the unbelievably painful season we just went through, and in many ways, are still experiencing.

But some of that prepared us for a future we never would have considered otherwise. And all of it is working to make us more like Jesus.

JASON MILLER: PASTOR OF ARTS & TEACHING

Like Tim explained, the last couple months of 2011 were awful. Really, really awful. On the personal front, I came down with a bug that went from bronchitis to walking pneumonia and lasted for weeks. I spent a night in the ER when a case of vertigo threw me to the ground on a street in South Bend and kept me pinned there, puking till my stomach was empty and heaving after that. It took a few days for things to stop spinning and me to get back on my feet. We got word that my grandmother was in her final days, about ready to give up the battle with Alzheimer's that had been taking her slowly for years. Our Senior Pastor's mom was in almost exactly the same situation. And there was the investigation we had to undertake at church, with the senior management team spending long days looking into allegations against a teammate and friend of ours.

I hated everything about that investigation. I hated the long days and sleepless nights. I hated having to second guess a friend and teammate. I hated the hundreds of hours that were stolen from the positive ministry efforts we lead. And I really hated having to make judgments when I know there will never be a day when I don't need grace.

One night, in the midst of all of that, just after we had delivered difficult news to our staff about our conclusions in that investigation, and as were delivering that same news to an auditorium filled with students and parents, I had a moment when my resolve cracked and a quiet voice inside said, "It's not worth it." In that moment, I felt that whatever joy or significance I thought would be part of the life I've chosen didn't compare with the frustration and heartache that apparently goes with the turf. The thought eventually subsided, and God was faithful in providing encouragement and replenishment after that difficult season, but that was a dark day.

In spite of how dark things were, there was at least one bright light in that season: going through that would have been so much worse had any of us had to endure it alone. But we had each other to lean on. Since my first day at Granger eight and a half years ago, team has permeated my experience here. We serve in teams. We lead in teams. And perhaps the most intense and valuable team experience I've had at Granger was during those terrible months at the end of 2011. I have even greater respect and deeper love for my friends on the lead team at Granger because of the dark season we endured together. I doubt anyone enjoyed that season in leadership and ministry, but I think we would all agree that, if there have to be days like that, we'd rather go through those days as a team.

THE END OF THE STORY

(REALLY, IT'S JUST THE BEGINNING)

I cannot overstate the power of having a clear and compelling vision. Whether you lead a large organization or a classroom full of kids, whether your position is CEO or parent or whether you pastor a church of a few dozen or many thousands—everyone needs a clear picture of the future.

It doesn't matter whether you choose the Moses Method (announcing the vision), the Team Method (gathering leaders to help decide) or the Crowd-Sourced Method (inviting the entire organization to participate). All of these have their place at different phases of growth. But it is crucial that you take the time to hear from God and chart a path to the future He is calling you   to embrace.

I'm not suggesting it will be easy. If you want to lead something easy, this ain't it. It is the hardest thing I've ever been involved in.

But I hope the story I've told will serve to give you hope and encouragement. I hope it will help you make sense of the pain you are in and give you some light for the path ahead. I'm praying that our story will help churches and organizations get unstuck from repeating the same conversations and arguments and behaviors that keep them in an ever-deepening rut.

If the kingdom of God can be advanced, even in a small way, through the telling of our failures and successes, then my mission will have been accomplished.

KEEP READING

The next section of the book will take you step-by-step through the process we followed to discover God's vision for our church. You're going to get half way through and think, "Wow, that sure is an arduous journey." Indeed it was, and there were days when we just about buckled under the details. But in taking every step, we were able to discover the vision God had given our whole church—not just the leaders.

Preachers like to repeat the phrase, "There' gold in them thar pews!" They are usually talking about money (shocker, I know), but we found it to be true when discovering God's vision for the church. The Holy Spirit is at work in the heart of every believer, and this process allowed us a chance to listen to Him through the voices of the congregation.

PART TWO: THE VISION PROCESS

CHAPTER 37

A PLAN

When we emerged from our January 2010 senior leadership retreat, we knew we wanted to take the time to hear from every person in the church about his or her vision for our future. That sounds like a good idea, but we had no clue *how* we were going to do that. I was tasked with the responsibility to come back to the team with a plan.

I started by identifying four groups that we believed we had to have represented if our vision process was going to be complete and inclusive.

Influencers – This included our entire staff and every volunteer leader in the church. It was non-negotiable that every person in the church who carried positional influence with others be heard.

Participants – Additionally, we wanted to hear from all the volunteers and those in small groups, Bible studies or other identifiable groups that gathered at any time for any reason. More than 50% of our congregation (considering average weekend adult attendance) volunteers at least once each month, and we believed no vision process would be complete unless all of them had an opportunity to participate.

Attendees – We then wanted to catch everyone else who attended the weekend service but who did not give their input as an influencer or participant.

Community – And, if possible, we wanted to hear from people in the community who did not attend Granger or any other church. If our goal is to transform the community, then it would be a miss to not hear from the average *Jane* and normal *Joe* in our community about their dreams for a better place to live.

I then recommended breaking our process into four distinct phases:

Listening – it would take us a few months, but we wanted to make sure we had enough time to hear from everyone who wanted to participate. This required enough focus so people knew we were serious when we asked the question.

Drafting – It was going to be daunting, but we wanted to consolidate the dreams and visions of thousands of people and write an initial vision document that captured the heart of the church.

Finalizing – Then, we would have a few cycles where we would send the written draft back out to gain feedback. This would help us refine the next version so it was more concise and clear.

Communicating – And finally, we would agree on a final vision that would become our guiding document for years to come. We would then begin to communicate that vision to everyone who would listen.

With these four groups and four phases as our guiding template*, we began a process that would result in bringing energy and momentum back to the church like we hadn't felt in years.

---

* You will find this template on pages 205-207.

CHAPTER 38

LISTENING TO THE CORE

There were several principles guiding us as we began listening to our influencers and participants:

- People couldn't be rushed.
- People needed to be able to brainstorm as a group *and* as individuals.
- People needed a way to submit ideas they might have even after the meeting ended.
- The leaders had to steer the conversation so it wouldn't turn into a gripe session.
- Everyone needed to know we were listening.
- The process had to be simple. If there were too many steps, people wouldn't participate.

Kem Meyer, our communications director, ran some test groups before we began training leaders, and she found that most people couldn't identify with the word "vision." Most people weren't running companies or organizations or didn't use the word "vision" when they were making long-term plans for their own family. She discovered, however, that everyone could identify with "dreams." So we changed our terminology early in the process and began saying, "Dream about the type of church you would want your family or your friends involved in 10 years from now. What does that look like?" In fact, we began calling it the *My Dream Project.*

At Granger, every group in the church is connected directly or indirectly to someone on our staff. Therefore, we started by talking with the staff about the vision and how important it was that we hear from as many people as possible in the church. That meant we needed to hear from every person on his or her team. That's a pretty daunting task if you lead our Children's Ministry and have 400 volunteers; or student ministry and have 200 volunteers; or guest services and have more than 600 volunteers.

But we provided a short training session and a couple valuable tools*, then gave them two full months to complete their task.

We said, "You shouldn't have to plan an extra meeting. It is likely you will already be meeting with your volunteers sometime over the next two months. We are asking you to take time in that meeting and ask your teams to dream about what this church could be in 10 years."

The various leaders were creative in how they gathered the dreams. Some took the entire meeting, gave a little intro talk and filled up whiteboards for 40 minutes while people dreamed.

---

*   Located in the back beginning on page 208.

Others made sure everyone understood the assignment, then sent each person home with a dream tool that they could do on their own.

Our guest services team put paper up all over the walls in their break room, and as the volunteers served through the weekend, they could come at any time and add their dreams to the wall. Our board of directors brainstormed on their own ahead of the meeting, then we provided time for conversation as a group. We didn't care how the ideas were generated—we just wanted to make sure they were heard and captured.

CHAPTER 39

LISTENING TO THE CROWD

By the end of April, there were more than 600 "conversation tools" completed and returned. Some of them represented as many as 40 people in one brainstorming meeting. Others included the dreams of just one or two people. Our mission was accomplished: we had reached every leader, volunteer, and group participant that we possibly could. It was now time to widen the circle to include every person who attended the weekend service.

We took a significant chunk of the weekend service in early May to ask the entire church to tell us their dream for the kind of church they'd love to give their lives to. Mark Beeson began the conversation by asking everyone to write his or her age at the top of the card—not how old you are today, but how old you will be 10 years from now in the year 2020. I wrote down 52. It's hard to imagine yourself 10 years older, and you could hear the crowd chatter as they considered that it really wasn't that far away.

Then he took a few minutes to talk about the impact a church could have on a family, an individual or an entire community. He asked everyone to take a few minutes in the service to fill out the card and write down the dream he or she had for the church. The card was self-addressed and also included an email address*. We received thousands during the weekend and hundreds by mail and email in the weeks following.

We were floored by so many of the dreams we received. It was humbling to hear how the Spirit of God was working in the lives and dreams of the people of God. Here are some samples of what we received:

"It's my dream that we double our current physical and online communities and that we start new physical campuses near and far."

"I dream the church will be a true cultural force ... one that breaks down barriers between people and spreads a viral infection of love in our community."

"I dream the people of Granger will continue to be the church outside the four walls."

"We offer to the community free clinics, free services, auto mechanics, free child care or counseling."

"A Community center that is available to have events, meetings, luncheons and more."

---

*   You can see an example of this card on page 211.

"Our church becomes a staple in the community ... a place our community turns to for help and guidance."

"We need a daycare for babies through sixth grade ... this way we can care for children in the community and share the love of Christ daily with kids."

"A place where reaching out to the needy becomes an absolute norm not a random act of kindness."

"Churches would be in schools, coffee shops, on the side of the road—everywhere!"

"Be part of a movement where businesses will get together in investing heavily into kingdom initiatives, pouring time and money into changing our country (nutrition, ethics, etc.)."

"Be available for important life moments and host weddings and funerals on-site."

CHAPTER 40

LISTENING TO THE COMMUNITY

We really wanted to find a way to hear from local residents who don't attend Granger. Our goal was to hear from the 60 percent who might never visit a church service—but as you might imagine, they are not on our mailing list.

Initially we planned to put up billboards all over town saying, "Tell Us Your Dream for Michiana."* But when it came down to it, we didn't have the money. So instead, we printed business cards that sent them to a website where they could answer the question: "Tell Us Your Dreams for Michiana in the Next Ten Years."† We handed those out to our people and asked them to give them out to friends and work associates who do not attend church.

---

* "Michiana" is the common nickname for our region, which comprises towns on both sides of the state border in Michigan and Indiana.
† See an example of this card on page 212.

We handed out about 4,000 cards and ended up getting responses from 60 people. The input was all over the spectrum. Here are some samples:

"Make downtown South Bend a place you can take the family."

"More gay people."

"Get the Mayor out of office and quit taxing the s*** out of everyone!"

"People caring for others and not just themselves."

"Jobs."

"More chocolate would fix everything."

I can't say there was anything that made it into the final vision, but we definitely felt the sense of hopelessness many people feel about their community. The church may not be able to do anything about the chocolate supply, but if the church is being the church, we should be able to see lower crime rates, more jobs and a greater sense of pride and selflessness.

CHAPTER 41

ANALYZING THE DATA

Now we had collected literally thousands of dreams from groups, individuals, leaders and attendees. But without some organization, it was going to be useless.

I asked my assistant, Theresa Hoeft, to pull a team together to organize the data. They discovered some topics that were repeated over and over. When the process was complete, we ended up with a 60-page, single-spaced document, organized into these primary themes:

Impact in Our Neighborhoods
Impact in America
Impact in the World
Chapel
Family/Marriage
Friends

Work in Downtown South Bend
Children & Youth
Personal
Education
Technology
Church Goals (basically everything else)

Our senior leadership team received the 60-page document, and we read through every single dream. It would be hard to express how encouraged we were by reading the dreams of our people. We had heard over and over how meaningful it was to our people to dream about their church. We expected that to some degree, but what we didn't expect was the impact it would have on us. God was speaking to us through His people, and we were listening intently.

As we made our way through the dreams, there were two primary things we were looking for:

1. We wanted to see if God was speaking to His people in the same way He was speaking to us. As we were in the middle of this learning journey of thinking differently about church, we wanted to see if anyone else was hearing from God in the same way. We were encouraged, over and over, to hear the people craving a church where they could discover their purpose and "be" the church in their areas of influence.

2. We were also looking for areas where God was speaking through the congregation regarding things that were not on our radar. We knew it

was probable that He might show us something that we had not even considered. And this happened! One notable area was the desire for a place to have weddings and funerals. We always knew that Granger didn't have good facilities for such events, but we didn't really see it as a huge issue. We've always used other facilities in town. What we learned was that it is very important in a healthy community to be able to celebrate marriage and bury loved ones in a comfortable place with people we know and love. Once our eyes were opened to this as a venue in which we could minister to thousands of people each year who were part of the 60 percent (those who would not otherwise ever come to a church), then it became key in the new vision.

CHAPTER 42

TEN-YEARS BECAME FIVE-YEARS

After the "listening phase" and as we began to analyze the data, it became clear to us that a 10-year vision was far too long to be practical. We came to this decision for a couple reasons…

1. Our previous vision was a 10-year vision. In hindsight, it began to lose its' potency about five or six years in. After that, it was difficult to keep the momentum behind what we still wanted to accomplish.

2. We thought back to the year 2000 and realized none of us could have predicted what ministry

would look like in 2010. We would not have predicted multi-site, nor 1,000 churches in India, nor a shift toward ministry away from "the box." And shifts in culture are moving even more quickly now. Ten years is just too long a time period to cast a realistic vision.

3. It was difficult for people to predict what would happen in their own families or jobs in five years and impossible over 10 years. If we wanted them to consider how this would impact their own lives, we needed to reduce the scope.

We believe even with a five-year vision, it will take great intentionality to keep our focus behind it. For this reason, we have divided the five-year vision into two-year campaigns, with a reboot of the vision after four years. It will look something like this:

- 2011 – Vision Introduced; the two-year *New Normal Project* launched to focus on first initiatives (I will explain this in detail later in this section).
- 2013 – Another two-year project will be launched to focus on finishing the vision.
- 2015 – Although only four years into the five-year vision, we will breathe new life into the church with a new five-year (2020) vision.

CHAPTER 43

FIRST DRAFT

Now that the dreams were gathered, we had the daunting task of writing a vision draft that was a compilation of our ideas and thousands of new ones. Wow, what a task! I knew I didn't want to do it by myself, so I did what any good leader would do—I delegated!

I asked each member of the senior leadership team to write a new version of the vision, using the 60-page document from the congregation's dreams and using the individual vision statements we had written back in January. They sent it to me and I compiled it into one document before our June 2010 meeting. If you look at the agenda for that meeting that I included in the back of this book, you will note that we took time for each of us to read through our draft. Then we went through each of our versions and marked them up with these criteria...

✓ = Must be in our final vision

X = Shouldn't be in our final vision

N = Neutral (could go either way)

This gave us great conversation about what we believed as a group. Following our two days together, Kem Meyer and I worked for several days to boil the draft down into one document. We processed it with the senior leadership team via email and in meetings during the next two months. It is hard to write by committee—so we would tend to spend our meeting times tweaking and critiquing. Then Kem or I would re-write between meetings and bring something back to work on again.

By September 2, 2010, we had a draft ready to distribute to the church. It was nine pages long, although only two pages contained our vision. The rest was a reminder of our mission and values, a list of frequently asked questions* and other supporting information to help them digest the vision.

The timing on this was perfect. Mark Beeson left on a three-month sabbatical on September 2, which gave us a perfect window of time to circulate this new vision draft through the church.

And that's what we did. During the next two months, the draft was distributed to hundreds of leaders through the church. We asked questions like:

What makes your heart beat fast?

What is confusing?

Does anything make you yawn?

---

*   I included the FAQ list on pages 216-217.

What parts of this cause you to say, "I'd love a church like that!"?

It was our goal to hear back from every single group and team that was involved in the "listening sessions" in March and April. We would not be taking this to the attendees or community, but we wanted to hear from every influencer and participant. We requested everyone to respond via email, and we received hundreds of emails. As the responses came in, we began to compile the common themes to find out what was working and what wasn't. We ended up with a 41-page document with feedback on the first draft.

It's important for you to understand that we weren't looking for a change in the direction. By this time, we were very convinced that we were heading in the right direction regarding the vision. We just wanted to make sure it was being communicated with crystal clarity. If there were terms that were not clear (such as "missional community," which we discovered very few people understood), then we needed to either provide a good definition or find a different way to say it. If there were portions that were making many people yawn, then perhaps it was too micro of a detail and we needed to take it out of the vision and include it later in an in-house strategy document*.

---

* You will find a summary of my conclusions related to the feedback to Draft I on pages 218-219.

CHAPTER 44

SECOND DRAFT

By the end of November, we began working hard on a new version. I wrote out a second draft based on everything I had absorbed from 41 pages of feedback and provided it to the senior team for review. We met several times and kept reviewing and revising.

Mark came back from his sabbatical, and we met for the first time on December 6. He reviewed what we had worked on while he was gone and added his thoughts. We continued to review it as a group on December 9, and within a week we had a second draft ready to distribute. This time, instead of being nine pages, it was only three pages (including a cover page with FAQs).

December was a busy month with lots of holiday activities and vacations, but we attempted to re-distribute this new version to as many leaders and staff as possible. We knew we needed every-one's feedback by early January, which wasn't ideal, but we were still able to get it to several hundred leaders. We ended up with 36 pages of feedback on the second draft.

And the feedback was getting much more positive! We knew we were almost there.

CHAPTER 45

FINAL DRAFT

In the early days of January 2011, Kem and I began to work off-line to take the feedback regarding Draft Two and massage the vision for our final version. We sent this to the rest of the team in time to review before our senior team retreat.

By this time, we had spent an entire year on the vision. We had included thousands of people; we had gathered feedback from leaders and church members over and over again. We had so much buy-in on the vision that it didn't require much time to finalize the completed document. We spent one day of our retreat focused on the agenda and then some time praying and thanking God for the process and the results. On January 20, 2011, the vision was complete. The work was done.

We knew we didn't have the money, infrastructure, staff or

leaders in place to start on every part of the 2016 Vision right away. It was a five-year vision, and therefore some things would receive attention right away, and we might not focus on other things for a couple of years.

We took the time before leaving our retreat in January 2011 to hammer out a schedule of priorities and sequencing*. This document showed us things that needed our attention immediately. It also took the pressure off for things that we did not need to focus on right away.

---

* This document in its original form can be viewed on page 228.

CHAPTER 46

COMMUNICATING THE VISION

Mark looked at us while sitting together on the final day of our retreat and said, "You might think this was a lot of work over the past year. But that was nothing compared to the work we have ahead to put this vision into play." And he was right. The work was just beginning.

This vision was going to require every person in the church doing his or her part. We needed to raise leaders and money (and fast!) if this five-year vision was going to have any chance of success. Our first step was in communicating the vision with speed and clarity.

We returned from our retreat and quickly put together a plan to communicate the vision. It included:

- A kick-off event we called the *Advance Screening**. This was our opportunity to gather all the influencers and participants and give them a sneak preview of the finished vision. We held an identical event on two separate nights so everyone had a chance to attend. More people came than we anticipated, and the energy in the room was electric. Each night ended with Q&A where people could ask anyone on the senior team anything they wanted.

- A four-week series called *Picture This*. The first weekend in February 2011 was used to give an overview of the 2016 Vision, and then we spent a week on each of the three main points of the vision.

- A 16-page "magazine" was printed to fully communicate the new five-year vision†. It was filled with stories, pictures and history and communicated the heart behind the 2016 Vision. This magazine replaced the weekend program for all four weeks during the *Picture This* series. I believe that print piece did as much to get the new vision into people's minds and hearts as anything else we did.

---

*   See the agenda for the Advance Screening events on pages 223-224.
†   See a portion of the magazine beginning on page 225.

CHAPTER 47

STRUCTURE FOR A MOVEMENT

Soon after the vision was complete, we began talking about how we were going to restructure the organization to accomplish our outrageous dream. We knew that our current structure was too complex and hierarchical to manage the growth of a viral movement. And yet, that is exactly what we were trying to start. In five years, there is no way we would have 2,000 reproducing churches with 100,000 reproducing followers—unless we completely overhauled our structure.

Today, the regional church (a term I'll use to categorize everything we are currently doing) is huge, and the movement (reproducing missional communities and essential churches) is very tiny. But in five years, we anticipate that more than 100,000 people will be connected to the movement and only 9,000 will be connected to the regional church. This can't happen under our current structure.

In May 2011, Rob called me over to his office to show me something he'd been working on. When I went in and sat down, I turned around and Rob had an entire whiteboard filled up with thoughts about structure. His recommendation for how we structure for a movement was brilliant. He proposed creating two separate senior leadership teams: One for the church, and one for the movement. The one for the church would remain hierarchical and continue to serve the regional ministries as it has done very effectively for years. On the other hand, the senior team for the movement would be very fluid, built to allow for low control and quick multiplication. Neither team would report to the other. They would be side-by-side, with a few leaders dually serving on both teams.

If you've read *The Starfish and the Spider*, then you are familiar with this concept. Though a starfish and a spider have similar shapes, their internal structure is dramatically different. A decapitated spider inevitably dies, while a starfish can regenerate itself from a single amputated leg. In the same way, decentralized organizations, like the Internet or Alcoholics Anonymous, are made up of many smaller units capable of operating, growing and multiplying independently of each other.

The authors also describe *hybrid* organizations that are able to operate both starfish and spider structures within the same entity. In essence, that is what we hope to create as we balance the missional **AND** attractional. We are committed to continue to reach the 40% while at the same time reorienting ourselves toward the 60%. It will require a *hybrid* organizational structure to accomplish this.

CHAPTER 48

THE NEW NORMAL PROJECT

As you can imagine, this new vision would not happen unless everyone got behind it. It would require resources unlike we had ever needed before. It is beyond the purpose of this book to give all the benefits and results of a stewardship campaign, but I do want to tell you a few things that made this effort unique.

This was our seventh stewardship campaign at Granger. For those of you saying, "What the heck is a stewardship campaign?" – it's a concentrated time when we talk about the vision of the church and ask people to invest financially to make a difference. My responsibilities at Granger have included leading six of these campaigns (1995, 1998, 2001, 2004, 2007 and 2011). In some ways, there were similarities between all of them. But The New Normal Project* was unique for

---

* Learn more at TheNewNormalProject.com.

many reasons:

- We didn't call it a "campaign." That's a churchy word that isn't helpful in the real world. When most people hear the word "campaign," they think of politics or war. Neither are images we want in people's minds when we are asking them to buy into the vision.
- We had just spent an entire year working on the five-year vision. The New Normal Project became the "face" for accomplishing the first part of the vision. By the time we made the "ask," people had been hearing about the vision for months.
- We had very few extra events (i.e. banquets, home meetings) and focused everything we could around the weekend services. People are very busy with very good things, and most of them can only give us one block of time each week. That doesn't mean they are unspiritual or don't love Jesus or the church. It just means they are living their lives, investing in their families and contributing to society.
- Instead of asking people to make a three-year pledge, we asked for a two-year pledge. These are uncertain economic times, and we know most people can't predict their financial condition very far down the road with any confidence.
- We took 24 businessmen on a vision retreat to California. It gave us a chance to talk vision

and hear their questions.

- This was our first project that focused squarely on the **AND** of ministry. No longer would we continue investing solely in reaching people through an attractional model of weekend services. This project would raise hundreds of thousands of dollars for a missional model to reach people through a variety of ways and places.

- The level of transparency was increased significantly. We had multiple Q&A venues to let people ask anything they wanted. And we didn't dodge any question.

- We developed a website and posted pledges and stories in real time. Rather than waiting for a big "unveiling" of the total amount pledged, we let people watch from their homes and offices as the commitments were made.

- We put together a two-year strategy for keeping The New Normal Project in the forefront of people's minds. We made plans, about every three months, to celebrate a win and connect it to the project. It was important for people to know the project wasn't just about raising money but was about investing it in people.

- Although it wasn't unique for this project, we partnered once again with RSI Church Stewardship*. They brought creative ideas, out-of-the-box thinking and substantial support to our staff through this fast-paced project.

---

* Find out more about them at RSIstewardship.com.

CHAPTER 49

IMPLEMENTING THE VISION

Now we are in the nitty-gritty of implementation. Perhaps another book will be written in a few years to outline everything that happened as a result of a congregation daring to believe in the impossible. As this book goes to press, we are only six months into our five-year vision and yet have already seen significant progress:

- We raised $3.9 million in pledges for the first two-year phase of the vision and have already received $2.6 million in gifts.
- We let some staff go who we believed were not going to be able to lead us into the future.
- We realigned our children's and student ministries and began taking steps toward a Family Ministry concept.

- We hired a director for our preschool and began making plans for a Fall 2012 opening.
- We made some strategic changes to more closely align all our campuses to truly be one church.
- We found the man to lead the training and launching of our Missional Community and Essential Church strategy.
- We launched a church-wide discipleship strategy to help every man, woman and student continue to take steps (wherever they are) while the missional community strategy is being developed.
- We transitioned our multisite campus into a physical building that will provide the opportunity to be a community center for its neighborhood.
- We launched a technology solution to help church members connect with each other and another that provides a method for leadership training distribution.
- We completed the design for the Commons and Chapel additions and began construction on the Commons.
- We took steps toward activating our Granger campus to have a community focus.

CHAPTER 50

AND OFF WE GO

We have just begun. There is so much more to do to see this 2016 Vision come to pass. But we are intensely committed to it. I've included many resources in the next section of this book, but if you want to continue to watch our journey unfold, I would recommend these two online resources:

LeadingSmart.com is my blog where I write a couple times a week about what I'm thinking, what is working or what is frustrating. This isn't a polished church newsletter—it's just my raw thoughts as they come to mind.

WiredChurches.com is Granger's hub for helping church leaders. You will find practical articles, downloads, workshops and conferences that include our most recent learnings. And if you can't find what you are looking for, you can always ask a question at info@wiredchurches.com.

PART THREE: TOOLS

GRANGER MISSION AND CORE VALUES
Affirmed at Senior Staff Retreat in January 2010

ON MISSION.
Why we are here. What we do.

Helping people take their next steps toward Christ...*together.*

WE VALUE.
What matters most along the way — these values guide our actions. It's how we get it done.

1. THE PEOPLE JESUS VALUES.

- Every person matters to God and matters to us - even if they don't know it yet.
- God doesn't love men more than women, the old more than the young or the strong more than the weak. God loves the "down and out," and the "up and out," and God wants everyone "out," in.

> *The Pharisees and their religion scholars came to his disciples greatly offended. "What is he doing eating and drinking with crooks and 'sinners'?" Jesus heard about it and spoke up, "Who needs a doctor: the healthy or the sick? I'm here inviting outsiders, not insiders—an invitation to a changed life, changed inside and out." **Luke 5:30-32** (MSG)*

2. CULTURAL RELEVANCE

- God's best is for everyone, not just us. We think like missionaries. We intersect people's lives where they live.
- If people don't understand what's being said, they can't apply it to the reality of their lives and won't be motivated to step toward the best life.

> *Even though I am free of the demands and expectations of everyone, I have voluntarily become a servant to any and all in order to reach a wide range of people: religious, nonreligious, meticulous moralists, loose-living immoralists, the defeated, the demoralized—whoever. I didn't take on their way of life. I kept my bearings in Christ—but I entered their world and tried to experience things from their point of view. **I Corinthians 9:19-22** (MSG)*

3. PERSONALIZED GROWTH

- "Healthy grows," and we want everyone growing closer to Jesus. Something is wrong if Christians aren't growing closer to love. God is love.
- Unity is not uniformity, and since one size does not fit all, the pastors will never be able to meet all your needs. Everyone needs his or her own personalized growth plan.

> *God wants us to grow up, to know the whole truth and tell it in love—like Christ in everything. We take our lead from Christ, who is the source of everything we do. He keeps us in step with each other. His very breath and blood flow through us, nourishing us so that we will grow up healthy in God, robust in love. **Ephesians 4:15-16** (MSG)*

GRANGER MISSION AND CORE VALUES
Affirmed at Senior Staff Retreat in January 2010

4. EVERYONE PLAYING THEIR PARTS

- The church offers easy access on-ramps for everyone because people need help discovering their roles and playing their parts.
- Everything's better when people participate using their spiritual gifts, heart, abilities, personality, experiences and resources.
- We do what we love when we can; we do what we must when we must.

Make a careful exploration of who you are and the work you have been given, and then sink yourself into that. Don't be impressed with yourself. Don't compare yourself with others. Each of you must take responsibility for doing the creative best you can with your own life. Be very sure now, you who have been trained to a self-sufficient maturity, that you enter into a generous common life with those who have trained you, sharing all the good things that you have and experience. **Galatians 6:4-6** (MSG)

5. TEAMS

- A team has external purpose. A group may not.
- The church is a team of teams, where the individuals that make up the team are as valuable as the work of the team.
- A team outperforms the individual in the long run, every time.

The way God designed our bodies is a model for understanding our lives together as a church: every part dependent on every other part, the parts we mention and the parts we don't, the parts we see and the parts we don't. If one part hurts, every other part is involved in the hurt, and in the healing. If one part flourishes, every other part enters into the exuberance. You are Christ's body—that's who you are! You must never forget this. Only as you accept your part of that body does your "part" mean anything. **1 Corinthians 12:25-27** (MSG)

6. CLEAR BIBLICAL TEACHING

- We ultimately trust Scripture because it is ultimately trustworthy.
- The Bible clarifies and articulates reality and instructs all life in it. When the Bible does not connect with real life, the problem is not the Bible; the problem is us.
- We make bad decisions with bad information. Everyone needs the Truth.

Understanding your word brings light to the minds of ordinary people. **Psalm 119:130** (CEV)

7. LIFE-GIVING RELATIONSHIPS

- Everyone needs to have friends and to be a friend.
- We celebrate successes, encourage next steps, forgive mistakes and call out the best in each other.

Two are better than one, because they have a good return for their work: If one falls down, his friend can help him up. But pity the man who falls and has no one to help him up! **Ecclesiastes 4:9-10** (NIV)

8. EXCELLENCE

- God demands our best. When we do our best, it honors God and inspires people.
- There is no reward for squandered potential, half-hearted effort or lukewarm faith.
- Excellence is contextual and looks different in every setting.

And whatever you do, whether in word or deed, do it all in the name of the Lord Jesus, giving thanks to God the Father through him. **Colossians 3:17** (NIV)

GRANGER MISSION AND CORE VALUES
Affirmed at Senior Staff Retreat in January 2010

9. INNOVATION

- We think big, take risks, embrace change and hold a healthy disregard for the impossible.
- The body of Christ is not an institution. It is a movement advanced through innovation.
- Innovation defines our response to challenges; it is not the objective.

*See, I am doing a new thing! Now it springs up; do you not perceive it? **Isaiah 43:19a** (NIV)*

10. LEADERSHIP

- Influence matters more than position, title or tenure. Influence leads.
- God doesn't do much without using a leader. Godly leaders are worthy of honor.
- Godly leaders demonstrate more than an ability to lead. They also demonstrate holiness and integrity.

*Teach believers with your life: by word, by demeanor, by love, by faith, by integrity. **1 Timothy 4:12b** (MSG)*

11. WHOLE-HEARTED DEVOTION TO JESUS

- The world won't be changed by half-hearted devotion; neither will communities, marriages, families or individuals.
- Unashamedly, we challenge people to fully pursue God. Love is a greater measure of devotion than religious zeal.

*Love the Lord your God with all your heart and with all your soul and with all your mind. This is the first and greatest commandment. And the second is like it: 'Love your neighbor as yourself'. **Matthew 22:37-38** (NIV)*

12. COMMUNITY TRANSFORMATION

- We love enough to pay the price to see the elimination of hunger, ignorance, disease, division, injustice, corruption, poverty, arrogance, hate, isolation, revenge and spiritual confusion.
- When the tide comes in, it lifts all boats. The more fully God's Kingdom comes, the better life is for everyone everywhere.

*My people will live in peaceful dwelling places, in secure homes, in undisturbed places of rest. **Isaiah 32:18** (NIV)*

VISION GATHERING PROCESS
Written 2-2-2010

Goal

Create a process to gather input from the highest number of people possible from our congregation and the community – resulting in a vision plan that will launch GCC into the next decade with purpose and momentum.

Purpose

Discover ideas, unearth synergy and create ownership for the vision that will launch our ministry direction for the next decade.

Four Groups

1) INFLUENCERS: Every staff member and volunteer leader.
2) PARTICIPANTS: Every participant on every identified team or group.
3) ATTENDEES: Every other person who regularly attends a weekend service.
4) COMMUNITY: Every interested person in the community (non-attendees).

Four Phases

1) Brainstorm/Listen (white-board, no ideas rejected)
2) First Draft (get feedback, find out where there is synergy)
3) Semi-Final Version (final feedback, express gratefulness for participation, invite to public unveiling)
4) Communication

MONTH-BY-MONTH PROCESS
Written 2-2-2010

This was our initial roadmap. We didn't follow it precisely, but it was our guiding document for the 12-month vision gathering and writing process.

	Influencers	Participants	Attendees	Community
	PHASE ONE – BRAINSTORM			
February 2010	Develop Influencers List with SMT 2/3,10 Ad-Council on 2/28			
	• Develop a tool to help every leader/group gather input. Include leading questions, easy way to submit, definition of a vision, etc. • Find way to track every person who is involved in the process.			
March 2010	Staff at SWAT on 3/3 Schedule additional leaders meetings (decentralized?)	Every identified group or team in the church uses the tool to brainstorm and record their input.		
April 2010		Continue through end of April		
May 2010	SMT (and others?) meet to refine, review, begin to draft Vision.		Weekend Service – take 5-10 minutes to invite feedback from every person in attendance.	Launch Community phase during Core Values series
	PHASE TWO – DRAFT			
June 2010	SMT begins distributing draft SWAT Influencers?	Use tool to gather input – does this make your heart beat fast? Is this the type of church you'd want to be a part of?		
July 2010				Invite anyone who responds to help us refine this through focus groups / town hall type meetings
August 2010	SMT begin finalizing into permanent format.		Weekend Service – take 5-10 minutes to read through draft and ask for input.	

MONTH-BY-MONTH PROCESS
Continued

	PHASE THREE – 90% FINAL		
September 2010	SMT finish semi-final document.		Gather Community Influence Groups for drill-down on emerging topics (i.e. educators, business leaders, healthcare professionals)
October 2010		One last feedback loop. "This is it. Before we unveil this to the church, we want your final feedback."	
November 2010			
December 2010	Mark returns from sabbatical and we do Christmas. With Christmas Offering, build anticipation for vision.		
	PHASE FOUR – COMMUNICATION		
January 2011	SMT finalizes vision at Retreat		
February 2011	Roll-out vision for the entire church in weekend series		
March 2011	Launch financial campaign that is directly tied to vision		
April 2011	Finish financial campaign before Easter (April 24)		

MY DREAM - LEADER'S GUIDE
March 2010

Twelve years ago, the people of Granger Community Church laid out a vision for our future together. That vision has largely been fulfilled! Now we are asking the entire congregation to help define the dream for our next ten years.

Why   Each of us at Granger Community Church is part of something bigger than ourselves.

1)   Every *individual is a subplot in the story God is writing through* **our church.**
2)   *In turn, our church becomes part of the story God is writing through* **each person.**

We want to help each person unpack and discover his or her thoughts and dreams about the future of our church. As we seek God and share our dreams together —we believe we will discover the vision God has for us.

How   You are a leader and influencer. We're asking you to invite and collect dreams from the people you're serving, leading and doing life with.

1)   **DISCOVER |** Brainstorm, dream and capture feedback. Some starter questions:
   - Dream about the type of church you would want for your family and your friends 10 years from now. What would that look like?
   - What vision could a church have that would be worth you giving your life to for the next 10 years?
   - How could a thriving local church help you achieve the dreams you have for your kids? Your career? Your marriage?
   - What might be some of the outcomes if GCC fulfilled your dream in 10 years?

2)   **CAPTURE |** There are no limits. From stories to stats to local to global, people express and articulate their dreams differently.
   - Avoid the desire to debate, analyze or redirect comments. There are no right or wrong answers.
   - Your job is to pull and capture ideas, not to build consensus.
   - Be ready to deflect negativity (i.e. "Our church has never been good at … "). Subtle comments like, "Let's keep this focused on the future" will help.

3)   **BE YOURSELF |** Honesty and frank conversation pulls people forward. Shake off the "fluff" and get to the authentic core of daily, cliché-free living. The conversation won't play out the same for everyone, but here are some examples of how you might get people talking:
   - At your next team meeting, take 30 minutes to "whiteboard" everyone's thoughts.
   - Meet your team before, between or after a service or event where they are serving.
   - Gather your friends around a meal, or schedule a team meeting.
   - Have a conversation with your small group in your living room.
   - Send an email invite with link to video from Mark. (10 minutes)

4)   **TURN IT IN |** The feedback only helps us if we get it. Be sure to record the dreams and turn them in so we can have the ideas of the entire church!

Mail 630 E. University Dr., Granger, IN 46530   ◆   email MyDream@gccwired.com   ◆   web GCCwired.com/MyDream

MY DREAM - CONVERSATION TOOL FOR GROUPS
March 2010

Over the next 10 years—what impact would you like GCC to have in these areas?

...in your personal life?	
...in your family or marriage?	
...in the lives of your friends who are not here yet?	
...in the lives of the next generation?	
...in our community?	
...in our country?	
...in our world?	

Name of your group or team? _____

Who led the conversation? _____

How do we contact the leader if we have questions? _____

How many participated? _____ (please attach names!)

Use this form (or equivalent) to collect the dreams of your group by April 30 and submit to ...

mail 630 E. University Dr., Granger, IN 46530 ◆ email MyDream@gccwired.com ◆ web GCCwired.com/MyDream

MY DREAM - ROSTER FOR GROUPS
March 2010

(This printed on the back side of the Conversation Tool).

Name of group or team?	
Who led the conversation?	
NAMES OF PARTICIPANTS	

Submit this Roster along <u>with</u> the Conversation Tool by April 30 to …

mail 630 E. University Dr., Granger, IN 46530 ◆ email MyDream@gccwired.com ◆ web GCCwired.com/MyDream

DREAM POSTCARD (WEEKEND)
May 2010

WHAT'S YOUR DREAM? WE WANT TO KNOW.

From: _____

_____

_____

PLACE STAMP HERE

1 **Write down your dream.** If Granger Community Church was having the most significant impact you could imagine ten years from now, what would that look like? For your family, your kids, your marriage? How about for our community, the country or the world? Tell us your thoughts on the front of this card.

2 **AT LEAST put your first name on it.** Your voice matters. If your dream is anonymous, it has less impact. All we need is your first name. But, you can use your full name or Twitter handle if you want.

3 **Send it in.** Drop this in the mail or in-person at any service. Got a big dream? Need more room? Bring it on and email *MyDream@gccwired.com*.

To:
MyDream
Granger Community Church
630 E. University Dr.
Granger, IN 46530

Back of postcard

MY DREAM BUSINESS CARD (COMMUNITY)
June 2010

IN THE NEXT 5 YEARS, WHAT WOULD IT TAKE TO MAKE MICHIANA THE BEST PLACE TO LIVE?

SPILL IT > Text *mydream + your message* to 62953 or email *mydream@gccwired.com.*

SENIOR TEAM AGENDA
FINALIZING THE FIRST DRAFT
June 29-30, 2010

Suggested Meeting Etiquette
- Turn your phones off.
- Keep your email program closed.
- Don't tweet.

We get so little time together as a team. Let's honor each other and be all here.

Goal by 5:00pm on Wednesday
- We have pulled into one document the essence of our first draft vision.
- If not written, we have an identified timeline/process for writing the first draft.

Things to Consider...
- A good vision statement should do the following
  - Help put feet on the mission statement
  - Provide new confidence in leadership and the mission
  - Generate fresh enthusiasm
  - Act as filter for opportunities and/or pressure to go a certain direction
  - Motivate involvement and commitment
  - Help build cohesiveness among staff and volunteers
  - Position the church for future change
- An effective vision statement will be:
  - God's will
  - Challenging
  - Visually Stated
  - Stretching
  - Emotional
  - Achievable
  - Clear
  - Focused
  - Future-oriented
  - Short
- Let's focus more on getting the concepts and not so much on word-smithing.
- A vision is not strategy. It contains a preferred picture of the future—not a strategy for how we will get there.

SENIOR TEAM AGENDA
Continued

Tuesday's Plan

- Pray
- Read each of our drafts (10 minutes each)?
  - No drill-down—but clarifying questions okay
- Break
- Re-read
- General discussion on all 6 documents
- Re-read and identify:
  - ✔ = Must be in our final vision
  - ✘ = Shouldn't be in our final vision
  - N = Neutral (could go either way)
- Discussion
- Plan agenda for Wednesday

CASE OF CONTRASTS
June 2010

I'm intentionally not including the early drafts of our vision document in this book, but this is one page from our first draft that all of us found helpful to communicate how we were thinking of the coming changes in a new way.

Chapter 1 (1986-2010)	Chapter 2 (2011 and beyond)
Get the community into the church	Get the church into the community
Church planting focus in India	Church planting focus includes America
Church defined largely by weekend service	Church defined by "where you are"
Centralized top-down structure	Decentralized organic structure
Primary stats are attendance and giving	Primary stats are community impact and "loving others"
Buildings serve the church—the community is invited to join	Buildings serve the community—the congregation also meets there
One central campus, 2 other gathering places	Hundreds of gathering places
No designated giving	Lots of ways to give to your passion
Everything branded "Granger Community Church"	"Granger Community Church" is just one expression in a larger movement
Facility expansion funded largely through debt	The debt is paid down to free up dollars for front-line ministry
Founded by Mark Beeson...led by Generation #1 team and structure	The beginnings of a transition to Generation #2 leadership and structure
"People shouldn't have to leave the church to do ministry"	"Let's train our people to leave the church to do their ministry"
Separate ministry to children, youth, and adults	A comprehensive family ministry that encompasses the entire spiritual development of the child and education of the parents

FREQUENTLY ASKED QUESTIONS
Distributed with the first complete draft on 9/2/2010

What is a vision statement? How is it different from our mission or values?
Our MISSION explains why we are here. Our VALUES talk about what matters most along the way—how we go about our ministry. A VISION STATEMENT tells where we are going. It gives a picture of what our ministry will look like if we are successful at a specific point in the future. The VISION is the finish line that pulls people "on mission" in a forward motion that is aligned with our values.

Is this the final vision?
No. We think it is close, but we are showing it to you because we need your feedback!

Why a five-year vision?
Planning is wise and biblical, it's what people give their lives to and rally around. We believe today's culture changes too fast to know what would be best for the church 10 years from now—but a five-year vision is both compelling and doable.

How did this vision get written?
In January, we began a process to gather input from the highest number of people possible— from our congregation and the community—to discover ideas, unearth synergy and create ownership for the vision that will launch the direction of our ministry for the next season. We brainstormed, listened, white boarded, texted, surveyed and gathered hundreds of dreams for how our community could be different because of our church. Every idea was considered. We compiled, organized and created this first draft based on the areas of synergy we discovered.

Can I show this to anyone?
You have a copy because you are a GCC leader. We need as much feedback as we can get from our leaders. If there are other leaders in your influence—we encourage you to show them as well and send us your feedback.

Mark is on sabbatical, right? Does he know about this?
Mark is leading the church on the mission God gave him. He has shared that mission with us, and it has become our mission too. He is expecting the people of God to keep moving the ball down the field and is praying the church is stronger when he returns than it was when he left. Not only does he know about the vision, he's been leading the discussions, and it is what he's dedicating his sabbatical to—a season of preparation, prayer and renewal. He's gearing up for a reboot.

What do you want from me?
We want to know your reaction. What makes your heart beat fast? What excites you? What part of the vision is hard to understand? What part of it gives you a reason for hesitation or fear? What parts cause you to say, "I could give my life to that!"? We need your specific feedback!

How can I prepare myself for the new vision?
Like Mark and Sheila, dedicate this fall in preparation for the mission. Do anything and everything you can to attend the AND Conference on November 4 & 5 of this year (register at GCCwired.com). It's significant to the foundation of our future together. Be poised, eager and open to change.

When will the entire church find out about this?
When Mark gets back in December, we will work on finalizing the vision after hearing all the feedback we get from our leaders. Then, early in the new year, we will begin to roll out the vision to the entire church.

9/2/10 Vision Draft – send comments to mydream@gccwired.com

SUMMARY OF FEEDBACK TO VISION DRAFT I
November 23, 2010

My Source: These are Tim's thoughts sent to the rest of the senior team based on his observations from the 41 pages of feedback combined with other personal conversations.

What are *MANY* people really *EXCITED* about?

- The fact that we are working on a vision. There is a real sense of momentum that has started in recent months, almost like a pent-up energy that is being released.
- The idea of *being the church* instead of just *going to church*. Rob's weekend message made that as clear as ever, and people are starting to get it. They haven't yet connected this to an organized *missional community*—but they get the "why" behind it. No one is questioning the 60/40 illustration—it's almost like they are saying, "Yeah, that's exactly right based on my friends."
- Building a chapel that will serve people in times of transition or crisis. Many people see the potential ministry involved in helping people through these major life events.
- Converting the Granger campus into a faith-based Community Center. I'm not sure they totally grasp what it means yet, but for whatever it means in their own mind—it is exciting many.

What are *SOME* people really *EXCITED* about?

- Serving the community with a preschool. People who are (or know) young parents are excited, as well as some who see this as a way to reach the community. Others see it as a stewardship issue of using the facility that God has given us.
- Launching additional campuses to reach our region. Many people bought into that vision nearly three years ago (when we planned to launch three campuses in 2008) and still hold to it.

What are *SOME* people *CONFUSED* about?

- A network of kingdom-minded entrepreneurs. Some are wondering how this works and whether the church will own for-profit businesses; others just miss the point completely.
- Sustainable initiatives to improve each domain in our communities. With a little explanation, people start figuring it out, but for many, it doesn't make sense without the explanation.
- Transforming children's and student ministry into a comprehensive family ministry. They like the idea of helping the parents but don't know what it means. The confusion may come mostly from current children's or student staff or key volunteer leaders wondering, "What does this mean for me/my job?"

What are *MANY* people *CONFUSED* about?

- Essential churches, missional communities, small groups, reproducing churches and the differences. Even from staff, where we have spent hours in training and conversation, there is still a sense of confusion. Example: In our staff Q&A led by Kem, hardly anyone could answer the question, "What is a missional community?"

What is **NO ONE** *talking about?*

- Not one person has said anything verbally—or in written feedback—about "training 100,000 missional Christ-followers." It's almost as if it didn't even exist in the document, and yet it is currently one of the core three points.
- Similarly, I have heard nothing about being "an unstoppable movement of more than 2,000 reproducing churches." Nothing. Nada. I think they sense movement but not because we used the word in this sentence. Also, the idea of a network of churches doesn't seem to motivate or excite people. Perhaps it is just a pastor-thing to be excited about that.

What **CONCLUSIONS** *have I drawn or* **QUESTIONS** *am I asking?*

- We don't have to put everything we plan to do in our vision statement.
  - For example, do we need to say "launch a movement of 2,000 churches" in our vision statement in order to do it? We can still have internal goals and metrics without having to convince the entire congregation of the importance.
  - Did we ever say (as part of a vision) anything specific that led to 957 churches launching in India? No. In a sub-point we said "we will offer opportunities for our people to make an impact around the world" – and through Rob's leadership, it resulted in 120,000 people meeting weekly in India.
- Should we focus our vision on the most transferrable, understandable, vision-inspiring elements (those which get people jazzed) and leave other equally-important but difficult-to-communicate elements in a separate or expanded *Under the Hood* document?
- This may be an over-simplification, but our vision needs to be for the purpose of inspiring, motivating involvement and raising money. There may be many things we SHOULD focus on that do none of those things.
- Some elements – like *missional communities* – won't be understood until they are seen, over and over again. As we elevate the stories, we will inspire new stories. Alan Hirsch tweeted this week, "You need a new story to displace a prevailing story." Right now our prevailing stories are mostly *in the box* stories. As we tell and celebrate more *where you are* stories, the story snowball effect will take place and pick up speed.

FINAL 2016 VISION
Distributed February 2011

The number of people being the Church in their neighborhoods, schools, cafés and communities seven days a week will outnumber the number of casual Christians just going to church.

- Every follower of Jesus has a "missional impulse" within them; we will help believers in the GCC family discover and activate this impulse to make a difference in their world.
- We will equip Christ-followers to leverage their leadership and expertise in every domain of society (justice, education, healthcare, government, religion, business and the arts).
- We will transition children and student ministries into a holistic family ministry, partnering with parents to disciple their children and students for 936 weeks—from the time a child is born until they turn eighteen.
- We will find, celebrate and tell stories of our people "being" the Church at every opportunity.

The differences at Granger Community Church in the next five years will be greater than the changes of the past twenty-five. GCC is not just an institution or location; we are a movement of people who understand we are Jesus' plan to transform and heal communities. We accept the challenge and we are raising the bar.

RAISING THE

BE the Church

B

FINAL 2016 VISION
Distributed February 2011

We will have remodeled the Granger campus and programs to help not just our congregation, but the greater community, with Jesus at the center.

- The Granger campus will become a gathering place for the community. We will build a chapel to help people through life-defining moments with inspirational architecture. We will build a Commons where people meet and friends gather. We will add paths, benches, pavilions, fireplaces and water features that invite people to enjoy the beauty of God's creation.
- We will utilize our fabulous Children's Center and launch a weekday faith-based preschool to meet the growing needs of parents as they try to raise their kids with virtue.
- Like Monroe Circle Community Center has done for a neighborhood in South Bend and like this remodel will do for Michiana, every location or gathering in our growing GCC network will exist for the unique transformation and elevation of the neighborhood, village, city or region where they are located.

FINAL 2016 VISION
Distributed February 2011

Every follower of Jesus will be a reproducing follower of Jesus. And every church will be a reproducing church.

- We will offer life-changing gatherings for worship and teaching in our current locations and launch three additional sites in our region with 9,000 gathering as one church in five locations.
- We will raise the temperature for life-on-life discipleship so it is normal for people to become reproducing followers of Jesus by owning their personal growth. Consumer-oriented Christians will, by design, not feel comfortable long-term.
- We will distribute high-quality content wherever and whenever it is needed. At any time we will be able to teach, train and inspire thousands of people as they gather from their home, church, business, or wherever they are located.
- We will launch and equip Granger Community Church start-ups all over the globe. All expressions—micro, mega, multi, rural, suburban, urban, multi-ethnic, local, domestic and international—will be united by the same mission and DNA. We will be a movement of more than 100,000 missional followers of Jesus gathering as 2,000 reproducing churches.

ADVANCE SCREENING - AGENDA
January 26 & 31, 2011

On Tables Ahead of Time: Blank 4x6 card, Vision 2016, Pens, Food boxes
Set-up: 3 Mics on stands around room for Q&A; 7 stools available on stage for Q&A, Music stand

6:30pm

1) Welcome (12 min, including 6 min table conversation) BEESON
   - Glad you are here, a great night ahead of us
   - Why you were invited: Core leaders, you don't think this about yourself, but you are one of less than 10% carrying the load.
   - Tonight is about launching (a new vision), listening (to your feedback) and leaning in (together).
   - Table conversation (on screen so latecomers know the topics)
     o When did you first come to GCC?
     o Why did you come back?

6:42pm

2) Current Reality (10 minutes) WEGNER
   - GOAL: Express excitement about where we are, but also talk about why we cannot stay here.
   - What God has been doing in recent history / where we are
   - Quick stories of transformation
   - Christmas Offering – amazing response
   - Recession / "real" reflection of giving in this climate
   - Reflection on the 60/40 – we can't expect everyone to come to us anymore. We must find new ways to reach them where they are.

6:52pm

3) Vision: dream for next 5 years (26 min) BEESON
   - 3 min INTRO:
     o Reminder of process—you helped us write this. You gave feedback, thousands of ideas and responses over 12 months.
     o Just completed last week – you are first to see it.
   - 3 min Read it all the way through
   - 12 min – Go back and spend few minutes on each section
     o We Will BE the Church
       ▪ Waltz – find a mic near your seat and talk about BE
     o We Will ACTIVATE the Campus
       ▪ Tim – find a mic near your seat and talk about ACTIVATE
     o We Will REPRODUCE at Every Level
       ▪ Rob – find a mic near your seat and talk about REPRODUCE
   - 8 min – Table conversation
     o What excites you about this vision?
     o What concerns, questions, fears do you have about it?
     o (Capture these on 4x6 cards at the table for later review, will help us refine our communication to the church-at-large).

ADVANCE SCREENING - AGENDA
Continued

7:18pm	4) The New Normal Project to launch this vision (25 min) BEESON

- 3 min Intro
    - o A 5-year vision seems huge, unimaginable, that's why we have brought it down to a 2-year project. We are going to focus on the next 2 years.
    - o It's going to take all of us working together. Some of you walk in this building and you have no idea that you are standing on the shoulders of people, just like you, who made a decision to give something up years ago because you matter to God.
- 7 min – VIDEO: Campaign History
- 10 min – here is exactly what we think we can do in the next 2 years, all of us together (on screen)
    - o 1-We are going to launch churches, sites, and missional communities.
        - One more regional site in next 2 years.
        - Technology to capture and distribute
    - o 2-We are going to build the Commons and Chapel.
        - (Picture)
    - o 3-We are going to open a world-class, high-impact regional preschool.
- 5 min – Table Q&A – what doesn't make sense, what do you wonder about, what would you love to hear the thinking behind? (Use 4x6 cards again)

7:43pm	5) Open Mic Q & A (35 min) SMT on STOOLS (Beeson moderates)

- Pull cards/select questions from tables, specifically vision/project questions that have been raised at tables in preceding conversations.
- Address as many as possible from front of room.
- At least once, focus on Elkhart – "Let's hear a question from one of our Elkhart leaders…"

8:18pm	6) Your Next steps (5 min) BEESON

- Be carriers of the Vision (bucket of gas/water)
- Begin praying
    - o about your financial participation
    - o for others in the church—the impact everyone can have in this process
    - o for those who will be reached/changed because of this Project.
- Save the Date: March 13th or 15th. (on screen)

Leave 4x6 cards on your table.

8:23pm	7) Dismiss – 7 minute buffer, need to end by 8:30pm BEESON

PICTURE THIS - MINI MAGAZINE
Distributed February 2011

PICTURE THIS – MINI-MAGAZINE
Continued

438 people were baptized in 2010.

Student ministry attendance is up over 25% from last year with 400 students involved weekly.

In a six-month window last year, we added an additional 250 churches in India.

[8]

PICTURE THIS – MINI-MAGAZINE
Continued

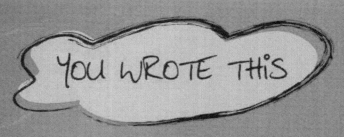

In 2010, we began a process to gather input from the highest number of people possible—from our congregation and the community—to discover ideas, unearth synergy and create ownership for the vision that will launch the direction of our ministry for the next season. These are a few of the word-for-word dreams that inspired the vision you now hold...

"It's my dream that we double our current physical and online communities and that we start new physical campuses near and far."

"I dream the church will be a true cultural force...one that breaks down barriers between people and spreads a viral infection of love in our community."

"I dream the people of Granger will continue to be the church outside the four walls."

"I can see us doing more with more campuses in Niles and the west side of South Bend."

"A community center that is available to have events, meetings, luncheons and more."

"Our church becomes a staple in the community...a place our community turns to for help and guidance."

"We need a daycare for babies...this way we can care for children in the community and share the love of Christ daily with kids."

"A place where reaching out to the needy becomes an absolute norm, not a random act of kindness."

"Be available for important life moments and host weddings and funerals on-site."

[14]

VISION PRIORITIES / SCHEDULE
February 2011

We made many assumptions about funding and staffing when we put this chart together. So changes happened later as we determined how much money was available and how quickly we could find staff, but this shows how we were thinking of the priorities and sequencing in the planning stage.

The Big Task	Who is Responsible?	Start	Finish
Being			
Establish coaching track for ministry start-ups	Rob	Jan 2012	Spring 2012
Make needed changes in current children's ministry	Tim	Jan 2011	Feb 2011
Restructure children's & student ministry under one umbrella	DC	Mar 2011	Dec 2011
Build a comprehensive family ministry with focus on helping parents	DC	Jan 2012	Dec 2013
Sustainable initiatives in seven specific areas of society	Rob	Jan 2012	2016
Stories will become one of the primary vehicles for our message	Jason/Kem	Now	Early 2012
Activating			
The Granger campus will become a gathering place for the community.	Waltz/Rob	Jan 2012	Sep 2012
We will build a Chapel to help people through life-defining moments.	Tim	Oct 2010	August 2012
We will build a Commons where people can meet / friends can gather.	Tim	Oct 2010	Sep 2012
We will add paths, benches, pavilions, etc.	Tim	Summer 2011	Summer 2013
Staff and program Chapel for weddings, funerals, etc.	Mark W	Fall 2011	August 2012
Launch a weekday faith-based preschool and/or daycare	Tim	Mar 2011	Fall 2012
Reproducing			
Enhance our I.T. technology infrastructure	Kem		
Enhance our A/V technology infrastructure	Jason	2013	2014
Launch additional multisite #1	Waltz	Now	Fall 2011
Launch additional multisite #2	Waltz	Spring 2013	Fall 2013
Launch additional multisite #3	Waltz	Spring 2015	Fall 2015
Essential Churches for the 60%	Rob	Spring 2011	2016
Missional Communities for the 40%	Rob	Spring 2011	2016
Identify / launch discipleship vehicle for those not part of MCs	Waltz (Rob)	Fall 2011	

ABOUT EXPONENTIAL RESOURCES

While the interest in church planting has grown significantly in recent years, the need for new churches has never been greater. Exponential is a growing movement of leaders committed to accelerating the multiplication of healthy, reproducing churches. We provide a national voice for this movement through the Exponential Conference and Exponential Resources.

Exponential Resources:

- Tell the reproducing church story
- Celebrate the diversity of models and approaches God is using to reproduce healthy congregations.
- Highlight the pioneering practices of healthy, reproducing churches.
- Equip, inspire and challenge kingdom-minded leaders with the tools they need on their journey to becoming reproducing church leaders.

For more information about Exponential and Exponential Resources go to www.exponential.org

TIM STEVENS

Follower   of Jesus. It's what guides his passion to ask questions and learn something from everyone. He never gets tired of it—dreaming and coloring outside the lines—always looking for a new way to communicate God's truth.

Husband   devoted to Faith, the woman who still gets his motor running after 22 years like she did the first time he saw her getting off the church bus in 1988. She complements his strengths and fills the gap.

Father   to four children in three different schools. Heather, Megan, Hunter and Taylor keep him running between college, high school, middle school, cross-country, choir, marching band, soccer, Lego league, the Apple store—well, you get the idea.

Pastor   on Granger Community Church's (GCCwired.com) executive leadership team since 1994, successfully blending innovative outreach and discipleship, helping thousands take their next steps toward Christ. He is responsible for a staff of 80-plus change agents who serve not only the local community but also hundreds of church plants throughout India.

Author   of the Simply Strategic book series with Tony Morgan and Pop Goes the Church. But, he doesn't stop there. Tim blogs about specific and practical resources at LeadingSmart.com to equip and encourage church leaders in an ongoing conversation.

Designer   of weekend service experiences and church buildings that help create the space for people to meet God. On his free time, he keeps it going with decks, home additions, and renovations. Carpentry and artistry are in his blood.

Strategist   who takes big vision and translates it into simple tools that help bring out the best in people and teams so they can soar.

Geek   who is an enthusiastic fan of technology, gadgets and basically anything that plugs in. Is it to a sometimes excessive degree? Nah, he still does his research and uses it to connect with people.

Connector   in the social world. Find him on Twitter @timastevens or on Facebook at facebook.com/tstevens